"Cat
Dancers,

by Ron and Joy Holiday
with Judy Ellis.

PINEAPPLE PRESS
Englewood, Florida

Inquiries should be addressed to Pineapple Press, Inc., P.O. Box 314, Englewood, Florida 33533.

Lines from "The Panther" excerpted from *Poems Since 1929* by Ogden Nash and used by permission of Little, Brown & Co., Boston, MA.

Excerpt from *Beasts in My Belfry* by Gerald Durrell used by permission of Collins Publishers.

Library of Congress Cataloging-in-Publication Data

Holiday, Ron, date
  Cat Dancers.

  1. Holiday, Ron, date-   . 2. Dancers—United States—Biography.
3. Holiday, Joy, date-   . 4. Animals, Training of. I. Holiday, Joy,
date-   . II. Ellis, Judy, date-   . III. Title.
GV1785. H59A3 1987   792. 8'2'0922 [B]   86-30679
ISBN 0-910923-35-3

Design by Jack Ellis
Composition by Hillsboro Printing Company, Tampa, Florida
Printed by Kingsport Press, Kingsport, Tennessee

To Hercules, Demetrius, Venus, Magic and all who have come before—you've enriched our lives so much.

Cat
Dancers

Prologue

The license plates on the cars lining our driveway and spilling over into the road tell the story of how fast and far news of our arrival in the neighborhood has spread. In less than a year, word that there is a couple with four performing jungle cats in the cattle-and-horse country near Gainesville has reached all over northern and central Florida. Today there is even an elderly couple who have driven all the way from Atlanta. What time did they get up to be in our yard at 9:30 in the morning?

This Saturday promises to be a typical Florida-summer scorcher, but the regulars come anyway. They hustle down the driveway and through the chain-link fence into the yard with the air of people going to a carnival. Newcomers who have never before seen one of our rehearsals fall into eager conversation with the old hands who never miss a show. Their excitement fills the air. "I hear the tiger is *huge!*" "Can we touch them?" "How far away will they be?" "The leopard leaps into his *arms?*" "Where's the best place to sit?" "John, bring the camera!" There are men and women of all ages and from all walks of life, many of them holding small children by the hand or babies still in diapers.

Every other Saturday, unless we are on the road or recuperating from a long haul away from home, we hold a rehearsal in the driveway. The practice keeps us and the cats on our toes, memories sharp, skills honed. We would do it without an audience, but even in the heat, or the cold, or the rain, the people come—to see Ron and Joy Holiday and Their Magnificent, Magical Big Cats.

In the cool of the garage, our four cats are doing what they always do before a performance. The tiger, all 550 pounds of him, is standing erect on all fours and rocking quietly back and forth—his way of warming up. The jaguar, feigning indifference, lies on his back, paws in the air, golden eyes half closed, ignoring the shuffling crowd and the occasional squeal of a child. The two leopards, one black, one spotted, sit serenely, front feet straight, heads high, like small sphinxes, waiting patiently for Joy to come through the door from the kitchen bearing a plastic tub full of chunks of beef—treats before the rehearsal, rewards for a performance well done.

Our warm-up is a time to break the ice for the newcomers in the crowd. I hoist Joy over my head by each leg in a split position and bounce her up and down a few times to loosen her muscles, saying, "Boy, you weigh a ton today," or "Be nice or I'll drop you." The crowd giggles.

They are relaxed and with us by the time I set up the tape recorder. In the second before our music fills the air, there is a moment of silence broken only by the distant squawk of our parrot, Pepe Taco, sitting in his cage by the window at the back of the house. "Hi! Hi!" He can't see anything but he knows what's going on and he is determined to make his presence known.

With the crash of a chord we begin. In fourteen minutes there is a little adagio dancing (lifts and splits and throws), a couple of illusions that leave the crowd gasping audibly, a ball of fire and an explosion of smoke, a leopard leaping through the air into my arms, a tiger rolling on the ground waving his feet like an overgrown

2

infant. Through it all we talk—to each other, to the animals, to the crowd. This is a perfect chance to make people aware of our concern for the conservation of all wildlife, and when the rehearsal is over and the audience crowds around to ask questions, we focus especially on the children. Here, today, perhaps a youngster can be taught that living things are sacred. People need to know.

As always, there is enthusiastic applause and then the crowd rises as one to get as close as they can to the animals. While I am busy rolling the cages out of the sun, Joy begins to answer questions. I pause to watch her contending with the crowd. Her white hair swings around crazily as she patiently responds to each while almost desperately making sure that nobody's child is about to explore a leopard's nose through the mesh of the cage. After more than 25 years of marriage she still amazes me with her energy, her radiance, that slightly hoarse voice with its heavy overtones of the Maine coast, those gorgeous dancer's legs. The people clustered tightly around her are awestruck.

An image darts into my head and then flits away, an image of a shy, skinny, lonely boy in a small town in Maine, seeking affection from the only life around him that doesn't judge: animals. And of a chubby, frizzy-haired, bespectacled, sickly would-be ballerina who seems physically incapable of strenuous activity but who has an iron will and knows she can do anything she sets her mind to. Places rush by, bits and pieces of Germany, Italy, Switzerland, France, Monte Carlo and its princess, Argentina, Uruguay. Standing ovations at Radio City Music Hall. Leopards, alive and dead. Punctured legs and shredded arms. A quarter century of almost constant activity, two lives linked together along a road that zigged and zagged but somehow ended up in the glitter of show biz. How lucky to be paid for doing what we love to do. . . .

PART
1
Making It

1

I was running down a dark New York avenue in the middle of the night with two garbage-riddled steaks bouncing around inside my underwear. Every few steps I gave them a hoist to discourage their efforts to escape into the legs of my waiter's uniform. It was February and it was cold, and I was running as fast as I could without risking loss of our first meal in three days.

It's a long way from mid-town Fifth Avenue to the cold-water walkups of Carmine Street in Greenwich Village, especially on foot, especially at night, especially in the cold. There was no money for bus fare or subway tokens. There was no money, period.

My wife, Joy, was expecting me home with my first paycheck, earned as a busboy in one of the city's swankest restaurants, and I didn't have the heart to tell her that it would be another week before I was paid. Nobody told me when I was hired, desperate for any work at all, that the restaurant discouraged frequent turnovers in help by paying only every other week. I couldn't break her heart, at least not on an empty stomach.

6

I had waited until the kitchen was empty and then rolled up my sleeve and dug the two steaks out of the huge garbage bin. My lean and hungry eye had spotted them earlier in the evening, when some dissatisfied customers had sent them back, and although it was an unforgivable offense to steal the food, I was desperate enough to risk dismissal. The steaks were dirty, and a small bite had been taken from each, but they would do, since our larder at this moment consisted of a small can of peas, a couple of slices of bread, and a bottle of ketchup. Not much sustenance for a man and his wife doing daily ballet exercise and trying to maintain a vital, youthful appearance in the hope of breaking into the Big Time.

We had come a long way from a tiny ballet school in Biddeford, Maine, but only in miles. Career-wise we were absolutely nowhere. How had we come to this miserable existence? What had happened to the high hopes and big dreams?

We had a peculiar history. As kids in Maine we had been forced not only into the same dance school (the only one in town), but also into constantly partnering each other. I was the only male in the school, a shy, scrawny, lantern-jawed kid from a poor family with parents who didn't understand. My mother tolerated this peculiar leaning of mine, as long as it didn't interfere with her budget. My father, from whom I had struggled valiantly to keep the dancing a secret, nearly went insane when he found out and all but disowned me. Boys who danced were fairies, and that was that. It didn't help that my real surname is "Guay," pronounced "gay."

Joy had started off with a far better home life than I, with generous and understanding parents. Born Doris Gagnon, she approached adolescence with virtually every physical shortcoming a girl could conceive of in her worst nightmares: Chubby, frizzy-haired, cock-eyed, bespectacled, she also suffered from monocular vision and its concomitant lack of depth perception. All of these attributes conspired to make her something less than a promising prima ballerina. But she had a will and a determination that set her apart from the apparently more talented students. Which is why we were stuck with each other from an early age . . . and loathed each other thoroughly.

As soon as I graduated from high school, I took the few pennies I had scraped together and made straight for New York, to study, study, study. I was lucky enough to land occasional jobs in the summer-stock performances of the hits of the 1950s—*The King and I*, *Oklahoma*, and the like. I had not planned on being anyone's babysitter, least of all for Doris Gagnon, but when she came to New York a year later, following in my wake, her parents had no qualms about asking me to let her share my ratty apartment. Everyone in town knew how we felt about each other.

Shortly after we set up housekeeping on either side of a discreet bamboo curtain, I left for Paris, hoping to improve my dancing even more by studying with the great Russian exiles there. I left dumpy Doris behind, to study as she could with the little earnings from her part-time job at a ticket booth in a local movie house. Not a total cad, I enlisted the aid of a photographer friend to keep an eye on her so her parents wouldn't worry.

Paris was expensive. I was able to find work off and on at the Folies Pigalle and Moulin Rouge, but the city streets seem to drain money out of me with every step. But it was exciting—an exciting city with exciting people and an exciting nightlife, into which I threw myself whenever I could afford it, or whenever I could find someone else to foot the bill. My letters home galvanized Doris. She soon wrote that she would be joining me. . . and could I please find her work at the Folies? I wondered how in the world I would convince the ballet master at the Place Pigalle to take on a short, chunky, unsophisticated American when he had his pick of the country's most gorgeous dancers.

I got the shock of my life when Doris appeared on my doorstep. Thanks to her meager income and my frequent transatlantic pleas for the odd twenty dollars to keep me going, she had had no trouble losing weight. With the chubbiness gone, she was downright svelte. The frizzy hair had been bleached to a platinum glow and piled atop her head, and the frumpy clothes had given way to a chic suit and spiked heels. She was stunning. She was also engaged, to the buddy in whose care I had entrusted her. I took one look at her and determined to woo her away.

Doris got her job at the Folies Pigalle and we set up housekeeping together, again. By turning on the charm, and by promising to mail her letters to her fiancé but flushing them instead down the watercloset, I gradually won her over. The ring went back across the ocean.

It was at this point that we began to consider turning our efforts to adagio. In the late 1950s this combination of ballet and acrobatics was the hottest thing in France. The standard act consisted of two men and a woman and a series of energetic and dangerous moves called lifts and throws. The woman was held overhead, or thrown between the men, in a variety of ways that required the precise timing of the trapeze, the balance of the high wire, the endurance of the marathon, and the graceful, muscular strength of the ballet. And a lot of courage.

We took ourselves to Monsieur Augusto, who was considered the best adagio teacher in Paris. He was a feisty little man, beetle-browed, bearded and intense, and he had no time for frivolity. The first thing he said to us was, "If you're not serious about this, get out of here." Once we had assured him we were genuinely interested in his art, he studied us carefully. Adagio dancers must be well matched physically: If the man's legs are a little too short, or the woman's arms a little too long, someone is in danger of hitting the floor.

When we left Paris in the winter of 1958, we had new names—Ron and Joy Holiday (taken from a romantic novel Joy had recently read)—and a unique act we felt certain would be a hit in New York. M. Augusto had put us through the mill, but out of his studio emerged an adagio team consisting of only two people and a series of pioneering lifts and throws that had never been seen before. One of these, for which we later became rather famous, was the toe stand, in which Joy balanced on my shoulder. One toeshoe-clad foot was on my collarbone and the other was lifted out and forward in a graceful and gravity-defying attitude. We also perfected a very dangerous "double drop" that many other teams imitated but never perfected. The double drop was traditionally done in two steps: The woman, stretched out flat as though lying on a couch, is held over the man's head and then dropped to his waist. There is a pause, a sort of quick regrouping, and then the woman is rolled out of the man's arms toward the floor. Done properly, the woman ends up being held by only a wrist and a leg while one knee is bent a fraction of an inch over the floor. The danger is obvious: If the man's arms are too long, or if he loses his concentration and bends forward slightly, the woman will hit the floor with a thud. On a dare, we worked out a way to eliminate the pause, and did the double drop as one smooth motion for years, without incident. But during the height of our adagio career, in the late sixties, we occasionally heard of severe injuries to dancers who tried this movement without understanding the risks. One woman required plastic surgery to reconstruct her face after she hit the floor and drove her jaw up into her skull.

I doubt now that our audiences fully understood both the effort and the danger involved in doing adagio. No one who has not tried throwing another person fifteen feet in the air and catching her on the way down, and *looking good while doing so*, can appreciate the strength and precision, the endless practice, the exhaustion, involved in doing just a few minutes of this sort of dancing. The concentration alone is enough to wear a dancer down.

So here we were, back in New York after a quick pass through Maine to get married before the families, full of expectations and high hopes. And why not? We were young, talented, and confident. My years in ballet and body training had produced an athletic, muscular dancer. My wife was a graceful, statuesque, platinum blond. We were attractive as hell.

Instead of finding ourselves the toast of the town, we rapidly became a couple of good-looking paupers. Which is why, nearly a year later, I had been reduced to working as a busboy and why I was now getting ready to clean up a couple of slightly used steaks. Joy, who had been lying cold and hungry in the bed when I came in, began to rise feebly as I set to work in the kitchen. I burbled a few encouraging words to her. "Boy, are we going to eat well tonight! Two beautiful steaks, honey, just you wait, they'll be delicious." But when I turned from the stove to reach for the meat, I nearly stumbled over her. She was sitting on the floor, tearing at the food like a crazed animal, her face smeared with ashes and garbage.

I stared at her for a second, rage boiling up in me against the unseen forces that had put us in this grotesque situation. I started to cry. Raising my eyes to the ceiling, I shook my fist at no one in particular and shouted, "You son of a bitch! If this is what this business is all about, I'm getting out! I'm giving it two weeks, just two weeks, and then forget it! Forget it!" Joy never gave me a glance. She was too busy ripping at the steak.

2

It was just as well that we found work before that two-week deadline expired, since I really had no intention of giving up. A friend who paid us the whopping rent of five dollars a week to hang his hat at our apartment when he was in town suggested we see a Mr. Moy at a Chinese supperclub, the China D'Or, in Times Square. Until that time, every club we had entered had been unwilling to risk two unknown dancers with an unusual act. What made Mr. Moy so adventurous we'll never know, but he auditioned us and then hired us on for two weeks. He didn't seem to mind that Joy was performing barefoot, for lack of money to buy the high heels that were a customary part of the adagio dancer's semiformal attire. We opened there on St. Patrick's Day, prompting Joy's parents to send a bouquet of green carnations, and were so well received that we got held over for a third week. With this sort of regular work behind us, I was able to quit playing at being a busboy, and we were able to attract the interest of an agent or two.

Not that we were on Easy Street. Our next big job was in the Catskills, at a resort called the Villa Maria. The bus fare up there for an audition took every cent we had, and when offered the job we were put in the humiliating position of having to borrow part of our salary in advance to get back to New York and pack. We had taken a hell of a chance; if we hadn't been hired, we would have been stranded.

The Villa Maria was small compared with giants like Grossinger's and the Concord, accommodating perhaps 200 guests in the large main building and in smaller cottages around the grounds. Behind the hotel was the Blue Mirror Casino, with a tiny stage just big enough for the musicians; the performers worked right on the dance floor. We worked there for the two peak season months of the summer, July and August, doing things we really hadn't been hired for. I, for example, ended up as the lifeguard, a job for which I was qualified only because I could swim. If I'd actually had to save someone, I probably would have been more of a hindrance than a help. Mercifully that situation never arose. The other thing we had to do that was odd was to push drinks on the customers, a distasteful chore not only because we weren't hired for the purpose but also because at this point in our lives alcohol was totally outside our experience (for one thing, we couldn't afford it). It was humiliating circulating among the guests at the casino with ersatz scotch concocted from water tinted with Coca-Cola.

We never knew what sort of situation we would find ourselves in. As relative unknowns with a precarious day-to-day existence, we were at the mercy of both agents and employers. Some of the places we were sent for "one-night stands" were terrible, with wretched working conditions. One agent booked us into a little hotel on the New Jersey shore, where we were met by a diminutive woman who was a cliché of the Jewish mama, right down to the heavy accent that was still foreign to our Maine ears. She was not terribly pleased to see us. "I tol' him I

13

don' vant a dance team," she shouted. "Vy he send you? Is no good, you go avay." Horrified at the idea of getting right back on the bus, we pleaded with her to give us a chance. When she relented, and showed us our working area, we nearly regretted her change of mind, for the theater was nothing more than a recreation hall and our stage just a part of the floor. No one sitting in the back would be able to see us.

But Mama had underestimated her audience's appreciation for good dancing. The three musicians were excellent, which really helped, and our performance that night was greeted with enthusiastic applause. As we stepped forward for what must have been our fifth or sixth bow, Mama came rushing between the tables and grabbed the microphone.

"You know vat?" she bellowed, "I almos' send dese pepple away. I almos' make a terrible mistake." Then she lowered the mike and turned to us. "You hungry? You got to be hungry. Come in kitchen, eat!" Matzoh-ball soup, chicken—we ate until we could barely move. We never knew how long a meal might have to last us.

We were still teetering between poverty and success when the winter of 1960-1961 approached. Food was no longer such a constant problem, but the apartment had no heat and we couldn't afford to rent a studio between jobs. This left us with the roof for practice, which was useless during bad weather. At least a roof has no ceiling to worry about. Ceilings are a real hazard for adagio dancers; you can't throw your partner fifteen feet in the air if she's going to end up hanging from the rafters. And the TV antennae on the roof made acceptable ballet barres. But it was dirty. After each session Joy was so covered with soot I had to scrub her down with scouring powder.

Late in the fall Joy spotted an ad in a trade magazine for a couple wanted to teach dancing at the Casa Marina, one of the fanciest watering holes for the very rich, located at the bottom of the country, on the tip of Key West. We knew we could handle ballroom dancing lessons but we didn't really have a nice, lengthy resumé and list of credits, so we invented them. We still have a copy of that creative letter Joy wrote listing all the wonderful places we had worked. We got the job.

Anticipating a long and luxurious sojourn among the rich and titled, I began to worry about Joy's bare feet. It simply won't do, I thought. We'll get down there, they'll see her working without shoes, and they'll throw us into the street. We still didn't have enough money to invest in an assortment of dancing footwear, but hidden away among our growing collection of memorabilia was a pair of old toeshoes, leftovers from our recital days at dancing school in Maine. I had always wanted to break away from the traditional high-heels worn by women in dance teams, to take advantage somehow of our years of ballet training, and this seemed a perfect opportunity to try something new. Without a word to Joy, I tucked them into our luggage as we set off for our last booking before leaving for Florida, at a nightclub in Pittsburgh.

Just before our music rehearsal on the huge dance floor, I pulled out the toeshoes and suggested Joy put them on. For a moment her eyes lit up at the sight of these familiar objects, but then she reverted to her usual practicality. "Are you crazy?" she wailed. "I've never worn these things to do adagio! I can't do it!"

"Do what you always do," I assured her, "and I'll take care of the rest." I watched her reluctantly tie on the shoes, fearing they would be too small after so many years. In fact, they were a little loose, because constant practice had driven her arch even higher than it had been in dancing school. She wobbled around on the shoes for a few minutes, still protesting that my trolley had jumped its track.

The music rehearsal went well, but right up to the minutes before our first show Joy was still fearful. It was all I could do to convince her that not only would she be able to handle the shoes, the audience would appreciate the balletic addition to the adagio.

Out came the ham in my wife. She got on that dance floor and she was in heaven. No one in the audience could possibly have guessed that the toeshoes were something new. A few minutes into the routine I stepped back to let her whirl about on her own. She started pirouetting and adlibbing all over the place, a glazed look in her eye and an idiotic grin on her lips. I began to wonder if she'd forgotten I was there. Finally I managed to sidle up to her and mutter, "Ahem, we do have a few more lifts to do."

After the show she crowed and carried on about how right I had been. The audience's reaction was fantastic. We had merged our ballet training and adagio expertise into something completely our own, bringing a new dimension to the act. And we could go to Florida with the assurance that no one would be offended at the sight of Joy's feet.

3

It was inevitable that we would turn our sights on Radio City Music Hall. Because of the tremendous crowds the Hall drew during its heyday, it was able to attract some of the best dancers in the country. If you were a tourist in New York in the fifties and sixties, you had to see Radio City; if you were a dancer, or part of a dance team, or a variety act, you knew that there were big bucks, regular employment, and a lot of prestige on the Great Stage. Auditions for the Rockettes and corps de ballet were held regularly; for everyone else, it was the usual matter of trying to get noticed.

There had been times when we couldn't even afford the price of admission. In the late 1950s, in our starvation period, we actually stole into the theater like a couple of kids crawling under a circus tent to see an adagio trio that was rumored to be one of the best. We stood across the street, shivering in a spring rain, holding one of Joy's gloves. When the show broke and the crowd began to stream out of the theater, we crossed the street and began backing into the lobby, looking anxiously at the

17

ground. Eventually an usher approached, and I went into a song and dance about not being able to find the other glove. The usher, naturally, suggested we go back to our seats and search there. We stayed through three shows, soaking up the atmosphere of the enormous theater and watching the famous trio like hawks to see what was supposed to be so wonderful about them.

It was a thrill to be in the the Hall but a crushing blow to our egos to see the adagio trio. They were doing with three people what we did with two, and their lifts and throws were nothing to write home about. It wasn't sour grapes on our part, either. Their finale lift, traditionally the one designed to stop the show, was our *opening* lift. Standing in the lobby after one of the performances, seething with resentment, I told Joy, "We can outdo these three blindfolded," and marched to a pay phone to tell exactly that to Radio City's administration. When Russell Markert, the producer of the show, answered the phone, I nearly panicked, but recovered in time to tell him that we were the greatest adagio dancers since the dawn of history. Then I all but begged for an audition.

Markert stunned me by agreeing. "Call my secretary in the morning," he said, "and make an appointment." We went home that night on a cloud. Was it possible that we had actually made a dent in those sculpted doors?

Reality returned in the morning, with the first in a long series of run-arounds. The secretary wasn't sure . . . Markert was out of town . . . could I call back again . . . she would let me know. . . . Over the next two years I nagged Markert mercilessly, sometimes even coming in through the performers' entrance and riding up in their elevator to invade his office and demand an audition. I lied to the doorman, saying Markert was expecting me, and made such a general nuisance of myself that Markert began to threaten me with the police. But my persistence paid off. One day, in the winter of 1962-1963, he threw up his hands in exasperation and said, "Okay! Okay! Be here tomorrow morning at nine in the large rehearsal hall. Tell the doorman this time you really *are* expected!"

This was too important an audition to face without the advice of our agent. At the time our routine began with Joy wrapped in two large ostrich-feather fans. The agent advised strongly against them, feeling perhaps that they were too "nightclubby." Whatever his reasons, we took his advice. After all, he knew best. Nothing could have kept us from the morning appointment. We were so excited, so sure that once the producers of Radio City Music Hall saw what we could do, there was no way they could fail to hire us. We performed the entire adagio, some 14 minutes, for producers Markert and Marc Platt, and by the time we were in our second lift both men were on their feet. Someone said, "Leon has got to see this," and a messenger was dispatched to bring Leonidoff, the "producer's producer" at the Hall. We performed the exhausting routine all over again. Leonidoff, appearing as impressed as his colleagues, asked if we could cut the routine to three or four minutes. I opened my mouth to bark, "Are you serious?" and then quickly swallowed my pride and nodded dumb agreement.

Everything seemed about to be neatly tied down, but then Russell Markert stepped forward and said, "You are very, very good. There is no doubt about your talent and your ingenuity. But you're so young. We're afraid you're too inexperienced to stand up to the demanding four-shows-a-day schedule here at the Hall." We protested that we were stronger than we looked, but to no avail.

Curiosity impelled us to buy tickets to see the show we had auditioned for. The plan had obviously changed, because instead of a duet the ballet featured a solo. But what held us riveted was the corps de ballet: Every girl had an ostrich-feather fan! "Damn," I groaned, "we would have been perfect!" Before leaving the theater, we called the agent—what we said to him is best left unrepeated.

We spent the next eight weeks doing club dates, dashing around the Borscht Belt and the big hotels, up to Boston, down to Washington, D.C., trying not to think about this greatest disappointment of all. But Marc

Platt had not forgotten us and one day, to our delight, he called about a new production he had in the works.

Platt's idea was for "living statues," two dancers in silver body makeup. We were to appear for only 3 minutes and 20 seconds, beginning at the top of a 12-foot platform in front of a "waterfall," an illusion created with the use of a new material, Mylar. Platt ran through a detailed description of his concept and then asked if we had any problems with it. "Ever worked in body makeup before?"

"Oh, yes," we hurried to assure him. In truth, we had never done any such thing. At the time it seemed like a small lie; we knew we could manage. He told us when to come back for rehearsals and costume fittings, and advised that we would be on trial for a day or two.

We rushed directly to a theatrical supply shop for the all-important silver body makeup. Back home, we painted each other from head to toe and set about learning what the stuff would do. What it did was clog our pores and turn Joy into a greased pig. There was no way I could hang onto her in the lifts and drops; she slid away from me every time. It was downright dangerous. We went back to Marc Platt and told him that we couldn't manage the living statues as he conceived them because the silver makeup sold in the States was inferior to the stuff we had used in Paris. Platt was undaunted; he promptly suggested we call France to order the "good stuff." Horrified, we quickly volunteered to look around in New York a bit longer before incurring such an expense for him.

We were lucky. Another supply store provided makeup with a glycerine and rose-water base which didn't clog our pores and which worked well with the rosin we depended on for a good grip. That problem was solved.

The next impediment was the waterfall. Platt's original idea called for both of us to be up there, but as construction progressed it became clear that only one person would fit on the platform. Platt reworked the number and came up with a splendid idea: Joy would dive from that 12-foot platform into my waiting arms below. It scared the bejabbers out of me, but Joy, ever the adventurous one, thought the whole thing was nifty.

We began by practicing off a staircase backstage at the Hall, with Joy diving into my arms from progressively higher steps, until she was working off the top, about six feet in the air. Not only was this nowhere near the height of the actual platform; what was more hair-raising was that the last few nails weren't driven into the real structure until just before the opening performance. We never did have a chance to try it out until it was too late to make any changes. We probably would have managed, somehow, if Joy hadn't thrown her back out just before the opening. In a last-ditch effort to avoid canceling out of the show, she hid mustard plasters under the silver makeup, trusting that no one in the audience would know the difference. But her confidence level was not what it should have been.

The moment came. As I waited below in the shadows, the spotlight hit the Mylar waterfall and Joy stepped out onto the platform. Even from where I stood I could see she was frightened witless. Only twice in her career has her pre-show nervousness failed to evaporate at curtain time. This was the first time. Between the butterflies and the pain, her entrance was something less than spectacular. She looked like a little girl at her first dance recital. And then, instead of a dive, she curled up and plopped off the platform like a sack of wet laundry.

We weren't surprised to see Platt in our doorway after the show. He wore a paternal air, though, and didn't seem too upset. "Ron, Joy," he began, clearing his throat, "that wasn't bad. It really wasn't bad. But it wasn't great, either. Joy, this is *show* business. You know, like showing off? There is no place for humility on the stage. Put your head up and be *proud*. The eyes of the audience are on you. *You are* the prima ballerina of this show!" We vowed to do better.

One of the other dancers in the show, a highly talented young man we came to work with often, Gene Slavin, played a hungry giant in a number just before our en-

21

trance. Among his props was a huge turkey leg from which he would pretend to tear a mouthful and then toss the leg over his shoulder, like Henry VIII. As he went through his number during the second show, he unwittingly threw the turkey leg up onto the platform, where it lay, an accident waiting to happen.

Joy appeared with all the presence demanded of her, head high, arms wide, the center of attention. Had she been looking demurely at her toes as she had during the first show, she would have seen the prop lying on the platform, but she stepped gracefully forward and . . . tripped over it. From my vantage point below I wondered if she had done the unthinkable and stumbled over her own feet.

Perhaps it was her desire to compensate for this clumsy entrance that now led Joy to execute a dive to end all dives. She left that platform with the determination and confidence of Greg Louganis, and it was truly a wonderful sight to see, except that, watching her launch herself into the air, I realized that she was going to overshoot me. I half-leaped, half-dashed sideways to be there when she came down, and mercifully caught her just below the knees as she shot across the stage on her stomach, gripping the floor with her fingertips and heading dangerously close to the footlights.

Back in our dressingroom, Joy was just remarking that her back was miraculously cured, when Marc Platt appeared again. He was a lot happier with Joy's entrance—and why not? She had practically killed herself—and he assured us that the vagrant turkey leg would be thrown off stage in the next show. But as he turned to leave he added, "Joy, try to tone down the dive a little. We can't have you flying into the orchestra pit."

Our performances went smoothly after that and, the trial period over, we signed the contracts that sealed us into the Hall for the run of the film. The first thing we discovered while doing daily appearances at Radio City was that the reduction to 3 minutes, 20 seconds was not a curse but a blessing. Suddenly we found out how exhausting four shows a day can be. Had we tried to do our full, 14-minute routine, we would never have survived.

4

We became fixtures of a sort at Radio City, appearing there off and on over the next eight years. We also traveled and performed all over the country, and in Europe and South America, working big hotels and small clubs, fairs and industrial shows, but we always dropped everything when Radio City called. It was a second home to us and we came to love the place and its people dearly. Bettina Rosay, the ballet mistress, was a particularly close friend and a great admirer of Joy. Many times she remarked that Joy was a breath of fresh air in a world of emaciated ballerinas, with her strong body and platinum hair. "She brings such glamour to the business," she would sigh. I couldn't resist telling her one day that years before a rather plump, inexperienced high-school graduate from Maine had auditioned for the corps de ballet and been told by Bettina that she would never have the strength and stamina to work four shows a day at the Hall. "That was Joy," I laughed. Bettina's mouth dropped to her knees. She had no recollection of the incident, of

24

course, since in her position she was passing out motherly advice to dozens of would-be ballerinas every week. I had undergone a change or two myself by this time. The most dramatic was my billiard-ball scalp. I'm a vain s.o.b., and I made up my mind while still in junior high school that at the first sign of baldness I would take drastic steps. When my receding hairline reached an invisible high-water mark, I got rid of what was left and purchased a collection of curly, and then Afro-style, full wigs. They really fit me very well, and the super-strong tape I use to hold them in place resists even the occasional cat claw. I make no secret of the fact that I am bald, but I don't broadcast it, either, and do get rather amused when people stand right in front of me talking about someone else's "rug" and saying, "I can always tell when someone's wearing a wig."

There have been occasional accidents, the most memorable occurring in Toronto, where, as the animal act we eventually became, we were invited to appear on a popular TV show, "Circus," which also featured a Mexican high-wire duo consisting of a rather heavy man and his younger brother. They were an impassive lot, and during our rehearsal they sat off to one side, arms folded on their chests, faces sad and almost stoically indifferent. In all fairness they were probably suffering from sleepiness, since the rehearsal was held at an ungodly hour of the morning. The time of day also explains why I didn't bother to use the strong tape that holds my wig firmly in place. Going into my "animal trainer" act, coaxing Joy to get into the cage, I did what I always do, cracking the whip on the floor. Once! Twice! And on the third snap the little string on the end of the whip caught in my wig and carried it high into the air, where it hung precariously for a second, for the whole world to see, and then fluttered limply to the floor.

There was absolute silence. The Mexicans' sallow complexions turned a sort of grayer shade of yellow, and if anything they became even more frozen in their chairs.

25

The producer's mouth dropped open. Nobody moved. Even Joy stood stock-still. Then I burst out laughing and bent down to swoop the silly-looking thing off the floor. "Hey," I called out, "no big deal. Don't worry about it." It took me several minutes to convince the cameraman, the lightman, and the producer that I really didn't mind, and to assure them that this sort of thing absolutely would not happen during the final taping.

Our lives settled down into a hectic routine of nightclub appearances all over the Northeast interspersed with the ballets at Radio City. We were soon able to abandon the wretched flat on Carmine Street and move into our own trailer in Bayonne, New Jersey, with a little garden and a view of the waterfront. We got a car, which relieved us of dependence on the buses to and from the Borscht Belt, where we performed constantly. Those were some of our favorite audiences—they were so full of enthusiasm and so willing to show it. They truly appreciated our work as art and told the hotel managers over and over how much they enjoyed us. It wasn't bad staying in these places, either. We were always given the best accommodations available and every effort was made to see that we were comfortable, well-fed, and had easy access in and out, even during holiday times when these hotels are jammed to the rafters with guests. The enthusiastic crowds were icing on the cake. We knew we could count on the audience for a warm reception, and they knew they could count on us for a first-class show. Some hotels even provided wooden clappers for their guests so they wouldn't wear out their hands. The audience would rap on the table or their glasses, making a wonderful sound, rather like hail on a wooden roof. One night a man got so carried away with his praise that he smashed his water glass to pieces.

We still have our records from those nightclub days, no doubt retained by Joy, the meticulous bookkeeper, for the benefit of the IRS. Sometimes we haul them out and are amazed at our endurance. One spring, for example, we appeared at the Sheraton in Pittsburgh on April 3rd; on

26

the 4th we turned up in Harrisburg; on the 5th we played the Statler in Washington; on the 6th, Atlantic City; on the 7th a double, the early show at the Edison and the late show at the Pierre, in New York. On the 9th we were back at the Statler.

It was in one of the Borscht Belt hotels, the Waldemere, that another performer said rather casually to me one night, "Say, Ron, when are you two booked for Radio City again?" Suffering from a terminal case of juvenile idiocy, I blithely replied, "Oh, in a couple of weeks." Joy nearly choked on her coffee. As we got in the car to drive back to New Jersey, she looked at me and shook her head in bewilderment. "Are you out of your mind? You *know* they just opened a new show there. There's no way we can be there in a 'couple of weeks.' "

"I know, I know," I apologized. "I just couldn't bring myself to admit we don't have another date there. I feel like a fool."

Joy nearly fainted the next morning when she answered the phone and heard Russell Markert asking if we could come into New York and rescue him. "I don't know what came over me," he wailed, "but I broke one of my own rules. I hired an act sight unseen and they're *terrible*. I knew them years ago and they were great, but they've changed drastically and they just aren't working out."

We raced into New York and were taken up to the viewing booth from which the brass of Radio City survey their productions. We were thrilled out of our minds to be in that room but we were quickly distracted by the events on the stage. Markert was right. The broad comedy of this team just didn't fit with the production number, which was *Scheherazade*. "Can you help?" he asked.

I requested a tape of the music and use of a rehearsal hall for two or three days. Markert went me one better and made a tape of the orchestra playing the actual music, so that we could acquaint ourselves with every nuance of the tempo. We had to work like fiends to learn the show and our music, but the following week the comedy team was out and we were in.

It was always exciting to be called for the Christmas show at Radio City, when the producers went all out to give the city's visitors a spectacular to remember. One of these shows was called "Joy Bells," a stupendous production staged by Russell Markert. It was performed under the lower limbs of a "Christmas tree" constructed by the geniuses in the scenery department. The huge tree hung over the entire Great Stage, an awe-inspiring sight from the audience. Our number was "Christmas Gifts," in which Joy and I were presents, she a doll, I a prince, concealed in enormous boxes under the tree. Gene Slavin, of the turkey leg days, was Santa Claus, dancing about to open each box, and throwing a little "magic dust" to bring us to life. Suitably dusted, Joy would step out of her box. My exit from the box was dramatic in the extreme, as the choreography required me to take only a single step and then leap high in the air before joining Joy for our dance number. That leap was so spectacular that photographers often waited for it, to catch me in mid-flight.

During one show poor Gene forgot his "magic dust," but he was a trouper and simply went through the motions. Most of the audience couldn't tell the difference. When he got to my gift box, I refused to move. No magic dust, no life. He thrust his hand at me once, twice . . . nothing. "Come on, Ron," he begged through his teeth. But I knew exactly how much time I could lose before failing to meet up with Joy for our duet, and poor Gene was in a sweat when I finally stepped forward.

In the winter of 1966 we received one of our greatest tributes, a request to perform with the Metropolian Opera Company. With Franco Corelli and Leontyne Price as the leads, *Aida* was scheduled for a single performance, as guests of the Philadelphia Lyric Opera Company. Since they were not performing on their home ground, they were free to choose whatever auxiliary artists struck their fancy.

We were asked to perform a pas de deux as part of the triumphal scene at the end of the first act, in gold body

The innovative toe stand. Joy mastered this attitude so well that she was able to do it aboard a moving ocean liner on rough seas.

A photographer caught me during "Planets," at Radio City Music Hall, in a perfect "six o'clock," one of ballet's most difficult attitudes.

Opposite: In 1958 I was lead can-can dancer at the Folies Pigalle in Paris.

Above: Doris Gagnon, at 16, as Salome, in he. Biddeford, Maine, dance school, and, *opposite,* at Radio City Music Hall 10 years later. Proof that anything is possible.

Training for adagio at M. Augusto's Paris studio. A complicated web of wires, bars and harnesses provided safe support for the airborne dancer.

First professional appearance, at the China D'Or in Times Square, 1959.
I am wearing a rented tuxedo and Joy is barefoot.

On television in Caracas, Venezuela, performing with the ostrich feather fans that our agent thought would be unsuitable for Radio City Music Hall.

Opposite: In performance at Radio City Music Hall's Christmas show, 1968.

makeup to match the opulent Egyptian sets. It was to be a brief appearance, a mere bauble, almost an afterthought. The curtain was to come down and that was to be it. But no sooner had we left the stage as directed than pandemonium broke out. Thunderous applause caused the curtain to rise again and we dashed out for a bow, to find most of the audience on its feet shouting "bravo" and "encore." The musicians had laid down their instruments to applaud, the maestro was chiming in by tapping the podium with his baton, and even the prompter was clapping. We bowed and bowed and bowed and then ran offstage again—to no avail. Somewhere around the 15th curtain call we dared to look at each other and found we were both crying, gold tears streaking down our faces. Joy managed to whisper, "If I died right now, I'd die happy." If our memories serve, we took 16 curtain calls that evening.

Between the acts Franco Corelli appeared in the door of our dressingroom. He was such an imposing figure, such a giant of the art, that I was quaking in my ballet slippers at the sight of him, but as I stepped forward to shake his hand, he embraced me and asked, "Well, young man, how does it feel to take all the kudos in an opera house?" I hope he didn't feel my heart pounding like a piledriver.

We floated off to sleep in ecstasy, but in the morning the critics threw cold water all over us. One wrote that the "unnecessary turmoil caused by the Holidays belonged in the music hall down the street." A couple of others pointed out that we broke up the opera because a great many people left the theater after the first act, figuring they had seen all there was to see.

Our spirits soared again, though, when we were asked to return to Radio City in the spring for not one but two shows, one right after the other. We couldn't have been more pleased about this honor, and certainly the steady income was wonderful, but it was also the most exhausting routine we've ever fallen into. The schedule called for us to be at the hall at 8 in the morning for rehearsal for the upcoming show, to perform at noon in the current show, rehearse again, do the 3 P.M. show, get a break, do the 6 P.M. show, rehearse again, and then finish the day with the 9 P.M. show. It all paid off in the end, because this time Russell Markert decided that for the second production, the highly desirable Easter Show, we should just be ourselves. For the five shows every day, the customary Easter schedule, there was no production, no corps de ballet, only the Holidays. We had the Great Stage all to ourselves, a performer's dream come true. It was a grueling routine but worth every minute.

Somehow we got through both shows and in the process set a record of 364 consecutive appearances at Radio City Music Hall, the equivalent of a year's work. The record stands unbroken today.

5

If we have to pick a time when we began to see the winds of change whispering through the entertainment world, it would be 1968. Violent upheavals on other fronts—the war in Vietnam, the drug culture, political assassinations, a relatively swift alteration in morality throughout the States—began to have their effect on the way Americans wanted to be amused. Ballroom dancing, which had been slowly dying since the beginning of the decade, was definitively dead, and the handwriting on the wall indicated that adagio would be next. Radio City was beginning its slow descent into obliteration.

The "Sin City" syndrome was no longer confined to Las Vegas: Topless bars and go-go dancers sprouted in major cities from New York to San Francisco, from Boston to Miami. This was brought clearly home to us when the phone rang one morning and Joy answered it. The agent on the other end offered us a very nice engagement, a three-city tour of California with a lavish review called *Les Girls! Les Girls!*, booked for the winter of 1967-1968. But there was a catch: Joy would have to perform topless.

31

Joy said nothing for a few seconds, and then she blew. "Are you trying to tell me," she said, very slowly and precisely, "that I have spent years and years working at the ballet barre so that I can dance with my top off? Let me tell you something: I don't have to dance topless. I've got something else; I've got *talent!*" And she slammed down the receiver.

In truth, we have nothing against topless performers. Many of them are truly talented people who have no qualms about appearing that way. There are many others, of course, who try to hide a lack of talent behind nudity, and that's another story. But for Joy there is no question: She has never worked topless and she never will. It simply isn't her thing.

In the end the producers of *Les Girls! Les Girls!* relented and modified the costumes so that we could accept the contract. But it was obvious that if we kept on trying to earn a living from adagio and Radio City, we would soon starve. We were in Mexico in 1969, touring with a small circus, and worrying about our future, when we met a pair of animal trainers named Billy and Judy Baker. They gave me the idea of adding a cat to our act. We look back on this moment of madness with astonishment. What in the world were we thinking? Did we picture a sort of oversized dog with the temperament of a tabby? Something exotic that would sit on the back porch and gobble up liver-flavored treats? An interesting pet that perhaps could be trained to jump around a bit and sleep on our feet in cold weather? We didn't have the faintest idea what we were getting into. You can take the cat out of the jungle, but you can't take . . . well, obviously.

We were making one of our last appearances as stars of the Radio City ballet when the call came. The movie we were supporting was "The Christmas Tree," with William Holden. It was therefore perfectly understandable that when the stage manager answered the backstage phone one evening and heard a man say, "This is William Holden, . . . " he chirped brightly. "Sure. And I'm the fairy godmother." And hung up. The phone rang for me again a few minutes later and this time the voice on the other end made it clear that the call was from the American office of William Holden's animal preserve in Kenya. Our leopard had arrived.

We were on our way to becoming an animal act. We were also in big trouble.

PART
2
Cats

1

We retrieved our black panther, Aladdin, from Newark Airport where he was crammed into a box barely
large enough to contain him. He was beautiful. And he
was fierce! We will never again make the mistake of buying a cat born in the wild, partly, of course, because the
laws now forbid it, but also because for all we knew this
animal had already killed his first meal.

While the federal laws of the time may have been lax
about two ignorant people buying a wild animal, the mu-
nicipal authorities would have certainly frowned on our
harboring the same in our residential neighborhood in
New Jersey. But we were able to keep Aladdin a secret by
the simple expedient of never letting him be seen in daylight. The basement of the house was two thirds above
ground, letting in plenty of air and light, and this is
where he lived when he wasn't upstairs with us for exercise and training.

Because he wasn't a kitten (or, more properly, a cub),
Aladdin did not take to us like a couple of long-lost
friends. He was so hostile that we had to feed him

through the wire mesh of his cage by putting canned cat food in a spoon tied to the end of a stick. This went on for three months, and then I came home one day and found him licking his dinner off Joy's fingers. From then on he was manageable.

Unfortunately, although we overcame the mechanics of feeding him, we didn't discover the problem with *what* we were feeding him until it was too late. We suspected that cat food was not a proper diet for a wild animal, but it was all the leopard would eat. During the several months that it took to switch him over to "fresh" meat, largely by sneaking the stuff into his canned food a little at a time, Aladdin was going through a crucial stage in his physical development. Disabling damage was being done to his system, and later we all paid a price for it.

Our ignorance was responsible for other problems, most of them far more obvious than the subtle effects of poor nutrition. Accidents began almost at once. Joy went to the basement one day to put the collar on Aladdin and lead him upstairs for his daily walk around the house, but instead of padding quietly along behind her, he suddenly jumped up on his cage. Instinctively Joy knew that trouble was coming, and she was considering what to do when she heard the phone ring. Knowing I would pick it up, she waited until it stopped ringing, and then lifted the receiver to tell me, calmly, that she had a problem.

But as soon as she turned her back on Aladdin he flew at her. Fending him off with a raised arm, she tore up the stairs and hit the kitchen screaming for help. Aladdin was right behind her and before I could drop the phone and come running he pulled three curlers out of her head, with the hair still wrapped around them. To this day she has three little places on her scalp where the hair will not grow.

Aladdin knew he had goofed and just before I stumbled into the room he turned tail and dashed back to the safety of his cage. Joy was a mess. "What happened to you?" I yelled at her. "Did the cage fall on you?" Joy didn't even realize that there was blood pouring from her head.

I poured mouthwash over her wounds, most of them in the arm she had raised to protect herself, got no reaction, sloshed on rubbing alcohol, still got no reaction. We know now that a sort of shock sets in, numbing the pain and even reducing what should be profuse bleeding. The real danger is from infection. We could not go to the hospital and explain that our illegal panther had attacked Joy, and our home remedies should have created pathological chaos, but this time we were lucky.

It didn't take us long to figure out that Aladdin was reacting to Joy's period. Over the years we have noticed that each of our male cats responds differently and we are extra careful around them at this time of the month.

Our first chore, after bringing Aladdin to the point of trusting us, was to acclimate him to backstage life, to walking on a leash, to the noises and smells of travels to and between clubs and theaters. The first time we returned to Radio City after Aladdin's arrival, I took him and his best friend, our shepherd Diamond, up on the roof of the Hall every day, for fresh air and exercise. There was plenty of room up there and the two of them rolled around and acted silly the way young animals will. I did this almost daily for about two weeks and then got a call to come to the office of Radio City management. The director apologized for disturbing me but he was rather exasperated. He had received dozens of telephone calls and letters from employers in the buildings that surrounded the Hall, complaining that the "odd silver man and his big black cat" were distracting workers to the point where nothing was getting done when we appeared on the roof. One caller said, "Hey, I've seen pink elephants, but this is ridiculous." "Ron," the director said, "do you think you could restrict your roof sessions to after business hours?"

For an entire year we made no effort to perform with the leopard. We didn't really know what we wanted to do with him, and he needed that time to grow and become used to our routine. Signs that he was capable of losing his cool became evident while we were still pondering ways of incorporating him into the act. I took him out for a walk on the huge stage of a Ft. Lauderdale hotel one afternoon, just to get him used to the place. The headliner, Victor Borge, was just sitting down to the piano to rehearse. "Do you mind if I walk the cat around a bit?" I asked him. Borge shook his head. "No, no, quite all right." I walked Aladdin to the opposite side of the stage and was on my way back, just behind the piano, when Borge unexpectedly hit a tremendous chord, immediately echoed by the orchestra. Startled out of his wits, Aladdin shot up in the air like a rocket and had an instant attack of diarrhea, which hit the stage floor even before he came down. He landed in it of course, and began doing what has become known in our little family as "shit-skating." Struggling to get the cat under control, I thought to myself, "If any of this stuff gets on Borge, I'll kill myself."

The placid Dane watched all this activity without raising an eyebrow and then muttered to no one in particular, "I hope I don't hit my audience the same way."

In our few passes at finding work with Aladdin, we met with considerable resistance. If we mentioned the cat to an agent interested in booking us, he would develop an ashy white complexion, mumble something about "liability," and back off. It was easy to understand. When we finally did land a job using Aladdin, in a haircolor commercial, the half-grown leopard really put his teeth into the act.

At first the photographer and his crew drove us and the cat crazy with their demands, expecting Aladdin to look wherever they wanted solely because they asked. Finally Joy discovered that the cat's eyes would follow Diamond wherever the dog went, allowing the photographer to yell "over here" and "over there" more or less at will. For long shots, the commercial called for the model, a willowy young thing half-bombed on drugs of some sort, to appear to be running gleefully alongside the cat. To avoid trouble, the camera was used to fake the angles, so that in reality the model was running behind Aladdin. Joy

39

gave her some stern warnings, chief among them, "No matter what happens, if the cat stops, you stop! Don't, I repeat, don't run up his back." Sure enough, Aladdin inexplicably halted in his tracks and the sweet young thing ran right over him. Aladdin promptly sank his teeth into her arm.

The damage was minimal. Unlike the cats that followed him, Aladdin was defanged, and the incisors in a leopard's mouth are quite small. The model required a stitch or two, clothing was strategically placed to disguise the bandage, and everyone went back to work.

We were still too dense to realize that liability insurance was a necessity in our new field. While we were filling in our time at a local club, Aladdin took another bite out of someone. The singer who preceded us on stage always ended her appearance by announcing us. She then walked off into the darkness of the wings, where we waited, holding Aladdin tightly on his leash. Night after night we did this until we could literally count the seconds between her last words and her footsteps passing us in the dark. One night she failed to leave the stage promptly—we'll never know why—and we stepped into the dark corridor just as she was walking past. She bumped right into Aladdin, giving him a proper fright. He in turn jumped up, sinking his claws into her dress and ripping it almost completely off her body. She also sustained a bruise on her arm, but once again we were lucky: Neither she nor the owner of the inn made a fuss, no one blamed us, and there were no repercussions.

We look back now, after years of cuts and bites and gashes and slashes, and marvel at our ignorance and downright stupidity about liability insurance. Eventually we did get coverage, right up to our little pink earlobes, but for more years than we like to remember, we were running about with our financial fannies exposed.

2

The man most responsible for encouraging us to put Aladdin to work was George Hamid, Jr., owner of the Hamid-Morton Circus. Hamid produced shows on the Steel Pier in Atlantic City, both in the Music Hall, which is the indoor theater, and in the circus ring at the end of the pier. Almost two years after Aladdin came into our lives, Hamid booked us to do our adagio in the circus ring. During rehearsal, we tied up Aladdin and Diamond nearby, where we could keep an eye on them and where they rolled around in idiotic puppy-kitten play. Hamid couldn't get over them. "Why don't you put this wrestling act into my touring circus?" he asked. We pointed out that the animals were not wrestling, merely doing what comes naturally, but he said, "I'm the one paying the money, and I'm willing to take a chance."

At Hamid's suggestion we went directly from Atlantic City to Maine and asked my father to build two pedestals. Over the next few months we worked ceaselessly to teach Aladdin a few relatively easy tricks. Unwilling to beat the animal or use any other intimidating techniques, we relied on the reward system. We began by putting the two pedestals quite close together, perhaps only two or three feet apart, with a piece of his favorite meat on the further one. It was nothing for him to leap that space and gobble the treat, and each time he did we said, "Good boy!" With lots of praise for each accomplishment, we moved the pedestals farther and farther apart, until, at about eight feet, the cat seemed to have reached his comfortable limit. During the training period Aladdin devoured his entire meals this way.

Something unusual was needed—a simple leap from point A to point B didn't seem very awe-inspiring. I finally hit on the idea of holding Joy over my head between the pedestals so that Aladdin could jump over her. I started by stretching Joy over the top of a barrel, far below the cat, until he became accustomed to the sight of her in his path. The barrel was gradually raised, then Joy was held on top of my head, no higher than the pedestals themselves, and then I began gradually lifting her. Unfortunately, when she was at arm's length, Aladdin simply used her as an interim step, leaping onto her stomach and from there to his treat. We were at a loss as to how to prevent this laziness until Joy suggested using the little flexible stick we call the "bopper." She feathered the wand in the air as Aladdin jumped, a technique we used daily until Aladdin expected the bopper to be there even when Joy no longer carried it with her.

After five months of training Aladdin, we felt confident enough to book ourselves into the Elks Frolics, in our hometown of Biddeford. Predictably, during rehearsal for that show, Aladdin refused to do anything. In the ten rehearsals we put him through, he did as requested only four times, but fools that we were, we went ahead with the performance, risking great embarrassment—not among strangers, but among people who knew us.

Playing the whole thing strictly by ear, we performed our adagio and then introduced the animals, praying for a miracle. When Aladdin suddenly and mysteriously recovered his memory and performed, we were astonished.

I held Joy over my head and said, "Aladdin, over Mom," and he jumped. "He did it!" Joy shouted from up in the air. The audience burst out laughing, thinking our surprise was part of the act. We showed astonishment each time Aladdin did a trick and the audience never did realize we weren't acting. This was esssentially the act we ran with for several months. We had it down to a fine art and probably would have never had any problems if I weren't such a smart alec sometimes. One of the little things Aladdin learned to do was to give me a kiss on command. The audiences seemed to lap this up, and when one group gave me a particularly enthusiastic response, I couldn't resist asking Aladdin for another. He bit me on the lip, and I bled through most of the adagio, all over a white shirt. It served me right. Aladdin's whole performance was based on expectation, on an unvarying routine. When I varied it, I confused him. Since that time we have been religious about ensuring that every aspect of a performance is exactly the same: the music, the direction the cages are facing, which side of us the animal walks on—every detail. Confusion creates chaos.

Not too long after we began to get regular performances out of Aladdin, we were back at Atlantic City, with Hamid's circus. Over that Memorial Day weekend, the headliner was Lorna Luft. We were very flattered when she came to our dressingroom one day and asked if it would be okay to bring in her sister. Something the Luft-Minnelli sisters said during their visit gave me the idea of dressing Joy as a leopard and having her disappear to be replaced by Aladdin as a finale to our act. I wish I could remember who said what to whom, but whatever. . . . Somewhere out there, Liza and/or Lorna deserves a tremendous thank-you for inspiring us to add illusion to our act.

I had absolutely no experience with illusion (or "magic" as it is commonly known by audiences), but our ignorance hadn't deterred us before and it wouldn't now. My father consented to help construct a basic steel cage which I then set about adapting, with a trapdoor and other devices that would allow Joy to vanish and Aladdin to appear in her place. Having no idea what I was doing, I just invented as I went along, and was surprised and pleased years later to discover I had accidentally duplicated a standard bit of the magician's repertoire.

One of the areas of concern was how big to make the compartments that would hold Joy and Aladdin. "How small can you make yourself?" I asked Joy when we returned to Florida, where we were now making our permanent home. She didn't know. Someone had given us a wicker laundry hamper as a wedding present and I suggested she practice with that. I figured if she could squeeze in there, it would give me an idea of dimensions. Leaving her to her efforts, I went into the yard to plant some bougainvillea bushes. At one point I heard her calling me, but my hands were full of dirt and I just called back, "Wait a few minutes, I'm almost done." A good twenty minutes went by before I returned to the house, to find Joy stuck in the hamper! She was wedged in so tightly I had to get a saw and actually cut the wicker apart to free her.

We finally reached the right proportions, although later, when we began using the jaguar for this illusion, we had to remodel the cage to allow for the larger animal. There is one big difference in the way we do the disappearance. Most illusionists will turn the "magic" cage around three or four times to give the partner time to disappear. With hours and hours of practice we have actually reduced the required time to *three seconds*!

The bookings we got with a trained cat and illusion got better and better. During one of these, at the Americana Hotel in Miami, we had the chance to purchase another cat, from a local animal exchange. We knew we needed a backup for Aladdin. He was becoming more and more important to the act, and we realized it would be foolish not to plan for mishap. The animal exchange had a pair but we could afford only one so, while we hated to separate the siblings, we bought only the male.

44

Antar, named for the father of a tumbling-act family we had met the year before, was five or six months old when he joined our growing family. He was so gentle that even Joy's mother, who is terrified of our animals, could hold him in her lap. She came to visit us at the Americana and on occasion would babysit for the young leopard so that we could enjoy a rare night on the town. Invariably we returned to find her sleeping on the couch with the black beast draped all over her.

Just before we left Miami, Antar suffered an injury at the hotel. Like Aladdin, he was crazy about the dogs and spent hours tirelessly chasing around with them. The whole menagerie was carrying on by the side of the pool when Antar slipped and slammed his shoulder into the ground. For a couple of days he favored that side, walking with a definite limp. As soon as we got home we took him to the vet, who felt that perhaps there was some damage to a radial nerve in the shoulder but suggested we monitor his progress by testing the feeling in his foot from time to time.

We installed Antar in the solarium/TV room where we could keep a close watch on him. For a while there didn't appear to be any permanent damage but then one morning Joy came downstairs to find the young cat foaming at the mouth, in a coma. He died the same day, from a blood clot born of the phlebitis that resulted from the injury. It was a terrible loss, but he hadn't been with us very long and we consoled ourselves by repeating frequently, "Thank God it wasn't Aladdin." The act could go on.

A couple of weeks later Aladdin began showing signs of weakness, diagnosed as anemia and undoubtedly the result of the poor diet we had started him on five years before. This was his condition when, two months after Antar's death, lightning struck the huge mango tree behind the converted carriage house we called the "cat castle." A large branch of the tree split off and drove through the window under which our big, beautiful cat was sleeping. He died of a heart attack.

Since Aladdin we have paid careful attention to our animals' diets and now feed meat and chicken alternately, enhanced with a vitamin mixture that is so effective that Joy dips into it now and then to strengthen her hair. Two or three times a week, and more often when the cats are performing, we give them big knucklebones to chew on. We must have the right combination because we have the healthiest, sleekest animals we've ever seen.

I was inconsolable about Aladdin's death and took to my room, sickened and grieving. Joy called in friends to sit with me and try to bring me to my senses, but for weeks I was a basket case and wouldn't even leave my bed.

I was just getting back on my feet when we heard a newscast about an animal breeding compound not far from St. Petersburg that was running low on funds and had reached the point of feeding its wards only every other day. We jumped at the chance to replace our cats, and came away with two for the price of one: a 13-month-old spotted African leopard we named Adonis, and a two-month-old Brazilian jaguar Joy christened Demetrius because, she said, "He will be my fighter, my gladiator." The choice seemed to make sense at the time; in retrospect we obviously had ancient Rome confused with Greece. It never seemed to matter to the jaguar and somehow the name suits him.

With two young, untrained animals we were forced to cancel a really choice booking in Puerto Rico but we didn't cancel a later date, at the Orleans County Fair in Vermont, in the hope that Adonis would prove unusually bright and receptive. By the time the fair came around we were at least able to transfer him from cage to cage, allowing us to perform the disappearing illusion. But he was otherwise fierce and intractable and could not yet be trained to jump between pedestals, walk easily on a leash, or do anything else before an audience.

We forewarned no one at the Vermont fair about the switch in cats, knowing that if we said we were coming up with a new, young animal the organizer would never believe we could pull off the act. When we arrived with a spotted leopard and a roly-poly jaguar, we simplified

46

everything by saying that Aladdin had died only days before and that we just couldn't disappoint the audiences and let the producer down and we had a responsibility and so on and so forth. No one complained. Ironically, Adonis was a far more effective animal for the illusion, because his spotted coat was dramatic in the spotlights compared to the way Aladdin had blended in with the black of the cage.

It wasn't until we returned to Florida, nearly two months after buying Adonis, that we were able to give him the time and attention required for proper training. On the road we had slept practically on top of his cage, so at least he was used to our voices, but he would not come out of the cage on his own. When the door was open, he would back as far as he could into a corner, hissing with fear. Once in our own yard, Joy began what proved to be a day-long effort to get him to take those all-important steps on his own. She placed his cage in the sun and his food a few feet away in the shade, and then literally talked him out the door, iterating over and over, "Come on, Adonis, good boy, Adonis, come on, Adonis," until she was hoarse. It took eight hours, even though he had not been fed the night before, but at six o'clock in the evening, hungry and tired, he cautiously stepped through the door and approached his food.

3

In 1975 Adonis suffered a horrible end, of which more later. He was replaced by Venus, a darling of an Indian leopard who was so small she fit comfortably in the palm of my hand. This was our first experience with a really young animal, and it proved to be very like having a baby—'round-the-clock care, but without the relief afforded by the occasional babysitter. Among the many items we had to keep track of was the regularity of bowel movements. Every time Venus skipped a day, we went into a veritable panic. In the wild, female cats stimulate this process by licking the cub's anus; we managed to make do with a warm, moist face cloth.

Venus grew to 90 pounds of lithe and agile feline. Perhaps because she is a female, she tends to be more high-strung than the other cats, more nervous, but by no means unmanageable. She seems to have a special affinity for me—she is as much my baby, my "Vee-Vee," as Demetrius is Joy's "Sugar Bear," a name which, she explains with a perfectly straight face, comes from the Latin "Sugarius Bearius."

From the beginning of our experience with big cats we wanted a tiger. This most awesome member of the family *Felidae* would make a spectacular addition to our act. But the timing was always poor. Most of the time when a tiger was available we were too broke to pay the price; on other occasions, when we had two nickels to rub together, there were no tigers to be had. In 1976, after returning from a successful engagement in Puerto Rico, everything fell into place. We got a phone call from Strupy Hanneford, one of the renowned Hanneford circus family, saying that she had two cubs, one of whom seemed to have the right disposition for a leash act.

We drove down to Venice to see the twin offspring that the Hannefords' male Siberian and female Bengal had produced. Strupy had named our candidate "Boomy." He was just five weeks old and did seem to have a very gentle nature. Joy picked him up, chastising Strupy: "How could you name such a darling little thing 'Boomy'?" We performed the "tummy pinch" test, tweaking the fur on the cub's belly. The average tiger will take offense at this violation of his person and hiss and claw in response. "Boomy" made that friendly greeting wheeze that tiger aficionados call "prusting." "Ffft, ffft," he went, almost smiling.

On Christmas day, 1976, the tiger, renamed Hercules, joined the family.

The process of acclimatizing a cat to travel and back-stage life is an extremely slow one. For months Hercules' only contribution to the act was to appear with us for a finale bow. Otherwise his cage was kept in the dressing-room for days on end, and only when he seemed comfortable there was it moved backstage for another period of time. Each move was designed to break him in very, very slowly so that nothing came as a surprise to rock his nervous system or make him distrustful.

In 1981 came Magic, a black African leopard, who is still growing and being trained to do whatever he seems inclined to do. Magic is our third black leopard. He seems little different from Aladdin and Antar, who were also African leopards.

Most people don't realize that there are several types of leopards. We were as ignorant as the rest of the general public when we first inquired about getting a cat. In our negotiations with William Holden's animal preserve in Africa, Joy wrote requesting a "panther." The response offered a "black leopard." Indignant, Joy fired back, insisting on nothing less than a panther. We were very embarrassed when we were gently informed that a panther *is* a black leopard.

Even that venerable observer of wildlife, Ogden Nash, failed to remark on the real difference between a panther and a leopard. He wrote, "The panther is like a leopard,/ Except is hasn't been peppered. . . . " Actually, it *has* been peppered. Up close, or when the sun hits his fur, Magic's spots, or more properly rosettes, are clearly visible.

It would be nice and simple to say that black leopards come from black parents and spotted leopards come from spotted parents, but the truth is that either variety can produce both colors, even in the same litter.

There is one more member of the cast who would be most irate if he were omitted from this family portrait. In 1969, while touring with the Mexican circus which inspired our move to an animal act, I made up my mind that I simply had to have a parrot. They were for sale in virtually every marketplace, but every time I bought one it died almost immediately. Joy kept telling me to give it up, but I felt sure that under the right circumstances I could keep one alive.

One day, bumping along a rutty dirt road in the jungles near Tampico, the circus' hired bus stopped beside a cola stand. As the passengers melted into the woods in search of private "bathrooms," I spotted a short, enormously fat woman standing across the road, calling *"parakitos, parakitos."* A half dozen or more baby parrots, birdnapped from their nests, were ranged along her arms. I stepped up to her, determined to make one last try.

My efforts to make a selection were somewhat hampered by the distracting sight of the masses of fat hanging from the woman's arms. Eventually, though, I pointed to one bird which, to my uneducated eye, seemed healthier than the rest and, taking a five-dollar bill from my pocket, looked the woman straight in the eye and said, "Okay. Now you tell me how to keep it alive!" The senora blinded me with a toothy smile. Tucking the tiny bird into her ample armpit, she dipped a bit of bread into milk in a tin can at her feet and then squeezed the little parrot until its mouth opened. With a thumb the size of a ball peen hammer head, she rammed the food down the bird's gullet. I winced but forced myself to pay attention. "Now," she said, handing the bird to me along with a little wooden cage, "you do this every morning and every evening for two weeks. Then you stop! Then you put the bread in the bottom of the cage and next morning, you'll see, there'll be little beak marks on the bread. No water," she warned, "no water."

It all happened exactly as she promised, and two weeks later Pepe Taco was feeding himself. He is with us today, a constant companion on our travels, a joy with his full range of trilingual nonsense—a little English, a little French, a little Spanish—punctuated with operatic cadenzas, whistles and chirps. He sits in a wrought-iron cage by the window, shrieking at the dog, laughing to himself, carrying on animated conversation with escapee parrots who visit the trees in the yard.

* * *

So our animal-illusion-adagio act, with one tiger, one jaguar, and two leopards, was complete. It has changed very little over the past few years. We appear in nightclubs, circuses, fairs, hotels, trade shows, virtually wherever there is work. Since it's expensive to haul four cats around the country, we try to avoid one- or two-night stands in far-flung places like Minnesota. Agents often get quite huffy when we turn down the short, distant jobs, but they don't have a 40-foot fifth wheel that gets, on a good day, five miles to the gallon, or a tiger who can pack away 25 pounds of meat at a single sitting.

The act lasts 14 minutes, short enough to support headliners in hotel clubs but long enough to stand on its own at fairs and trade shows. Joy and I do a few minutes of adagio, I in a "lion tamer" costume, she in a leopard-printed bikini with matching cap adorned with cat's ears. I "urge" her into the magic cage with a few snaps of the whip, cover the cage, count to three, uncover, and voilà! There sits Demetrius. The speed of Joy's disappearance is what makes this illusion so spectacular; invariably an audible gasp of amazement ripples through the audience.

I lead Demetrius around the stage, showing him off to the audience, and then, suddenly, Joy remerges in the cage, pulls the cover off, and steps out—wearing a completely different costume! She then leads Demetrius through his sit-up on the smaller of our two mirrored balls. The jaguar has beautiful markings on his stomach—a portion of his anatomy that few people ever get a chance to see—and he looks spectacular when the lights hit him and the mirrors flash on the rotating ball.

Venus' contribution to the act is her astonishing 20-foot leap from the mirror ball into my arms. Leopards are natural leapers, so it's no effort for her to jump that far. What was difficult was training her to do it on command. Even after she seemed to have the leap down pat, there were occasions when something would set her off—a distraction in the wings (dogs in particular make her very uncomfortable) or an unusually noisy audience.

Magic's part of the act involves what is known in the trade as a "cremation." Joy steps into a large mirror ball, the lid is lowered on her, and then I set the ball afire. When the flames die down, I pull back the lid and Magic emerges. After showing him off to the audience and leading him to jump up on a cage and give me a few kisses, I hoist him up on my shoulders (where he looks quite spectacular in contrast to my white costume) and remind the audience that "this is the only way people should wear furs." Magic is then returned to a corner cage, where I make a great show of stuffing his enormous tail in behind him. Back at the mirror ball, I set off a flash of smoke, at which point Joy reemerges, again in a totally different costume.

During the act we also perform a levitation, in which Joy rises from a couch, flat on her back, straight into the air.

Hercules we save for last. Joy makes a little speech about each animal and then asks the audience if they would like to meet the "baby" of the family, whereupon I lead Hercules in from the wings. He is so big and looks so beautiful in the stage lights that the audience oohs and aahs every time. Hercules sits up and rolls over, on command, and also does something that for years was thought impossible. The mythology had it that lying supine in front of a big cat was an invitation to disaster, that the cat would be unable to resist attacking someone in such a vulnerable position. We have definitely proved this theory to be hokum, because near the end of every performance Joy lies down on her back on the stage and Hercules lowers himself across her midsection. He has never shown any inclination to do anything but what's expected of him. The only problem, and this may simply be a sense of humor in an animal not known for having one, is that despite my constant efforts to steer him to Joy's waist, at the last moment he invariably shifts to the left and lies on her chest! I don't know if the audience can hear the "Oooff" that Joy always let out when he does this. It can be quite painful, since Hercules weighs about 550 pounds.

Our act ends with Joy riding off stage on Hercules' back, wearing a cowboy hat, then returning to kiss me behind the raised hat as the lights go down. In the black, we leave the stage.

* * *

When we began working with Aladdin, our ignorance was enormous. Looking back, we realize that we made remarkable progress, especially since there was no one to help us. With the first trick, teaching Aladdin to jump between pedastals while I held Joy over my head, I had nothing to use but my voice as encouragement. Aladdin's collar was linked by a long leash to a belt around my waist, so he couldn't run off, but otherwise he could do whatever he wanted, including nothing.

Pain would have accelerated the training process enormously, but we made a conscious decision from the start to eschew the traditional "train-with-pain" method. Even though the reward system is excrutiatingly slow, and even though we are in a very small minority of non-traditional trainers, we cannot and will not inflict pain on a living creature. Our respect for animals, our ecological concerns for wildlife, our genuine love for the pets are rooted deep in our childhoods, and no need for time or money can rattle those foundations. Animals provided precious escape for me when I was very young. By the time I was twelve I had trained a cat to do the sort of tricks normally coaxed out of dogs. I had a pet goose, as well as a crow and a hawk who answered to my call. Like many an unhappy child, I sought companions among those who do not judge. While Joy's love of animals springs from healthier sources—a respect for and tolerance of all life learned in a warm, affectionate and religious family—it is a devotion as fundamental and as unshakable as mine. We are often chided by other trainers for being "soft," but we get our own back every time one of our pets slobbers us with kisses, and we sleep well at night.

I won't go into the details of the nasty things a lot of trainers do to intimidate their animals into submission and obedience. Suffice to repeat the following conversation, which occurred at a reputable establishment where we were following close on the heels of a far better known animal act than ours:

STAGE MANAGER: "Ron, where do you want your electrical outlets?"

RON: "Well, let's see. We'll need one there, for the two mirror balls, and another there, for the levitation. . . . "

STAGE MANAGER: "Okay, but where do you want the electricity for the cages?"

RON: "Cages?"

STAGE MANAGER: "Yeah, you know, to the bottoms of the cages."

I'm a little dense. It took the stage manager a while to make me realize that some illusionists "motivate" caged cats by electrical shock to their feet.

We can hardly ever get through an appearance without being graphically reminded of the differences between our training methods and those of most other animal acts. In the first place, it must be remembered that "arena acts," the traditional enclosed cage with a trainer, a dozen cats, and assorted jumping equipment, must have fierce-looking animals or the whole point is lost. All too often, unfortunately, the "acting" that a lion or tiger is doing in that cage, of hissing, snarling and making attempts to claw the trainer, is anything but an act. Our act, which is called a "leash act," requires just the opposite temperament in the animals: docility, "cuteness," evenness of temper. I'm not sure whether we ended up with a leash act because we wouldn't train our cats to be ferocious, or whether we made a conscious move to avoid having to produce even a falsely fierce animal. Whatever.

There is a very practical side to the reward system of training, which is cousin to our practice of never asking an animal to do something that goes against his nature. The use of pain, or forcing a tiger, for example, to leap through a full circle of flame, sometimes shortens the lifespan. It isn't difficult to imagine the strain on an animal's heart inflicted by daily exposure to fear.

Another bone of constant contention is cleanliness. Our cages are kept as clean and scentless as possible. We have seen far too many acts in our travels where the animals are kept pent up for days in a small cage, living in their own filth and without exercise. Every time we encounter a trainer who indulges in this sort of neglect, we go insane. Joy in particular has no qualms whatsoever about walking up to a total stranger and giving him or her a lengthy lecture on proper care of wild animals. Somehow, she gets away with it; often the poor slob on the receiving side of the discussion ends up thanking her.

I'm confident that if I tried giving a total stranger hell, I'd get nothing for my trouble but a black eye.

In the early 1980s, a tour of eastern Canada with Ian Garden's circus afforded our cats their first exposure to other animals—large, smelly, noisy, unhappy animals. The lions in the arena act, having been cooped up in their trailer for days on end, sent our cats into a frenzy with their constant whines and roars. On the morning of the first day, as we were unloading our van, Joy took one look at Demi and said, "That's it, we're not using him." The frightened jaguar was trying to dig his way out of his cage, clawing frantically at the floor.

What with the confusion of a new place, a shortage of rehearsal time, and the discontented animals around us, the opening show was a disaster from start to finish, not just for us, but for most of the animal acts. Some of the dogs in Garden's own act bolted out of the arena, as did his son's ponies. Most of the animals left their mark on the floor.

For the first time in years our cats found themselves working under houselights, which allow them to see the audience and the constant to-ing and fro-ing of the butchers, with their drinks and cotton candy and, worst of all, balloons. After days of traveling in the trailer, the cats were now asked to just plunge right in and do their thing. They balked—all of them.

Our leaping leopard refused to leap. The tiger refused to come out of his cage. I was too busy trying to hold things together to be embarrassed, although after we left the ring I wanted to drop through the floor. Joy did what she always does after a bad show—she got sick to her stomach, and cried a lot.

Other trainers in this situation can resort to the application of fear to get their animals moving, fear sufficient to overcome the animal's already near-hysterical state. We could not, would not, will not. In this particular circus we were lucky enough to have the full support of the owner, who assured us that he knew what we could do, that everyone was having trouble, that all would be

56

well by the second day. Joy, whimpering through her tears, remarked that she certainly hoped so, because, if not, she was going to quit the business and become a waitress.

On the second day we finally had a chance to rehearse the jaguar. The arena trainer, who had been getting a daily earful from Joy about the cleanliness of his cages, popped in to watch, and made the mistake of criticizing Demi's sit-up. The jaguar didn't hold his paws high enough for this man's standards. I couldn't resist pointing out to the man that while his animals were wonderfully fierce on stage, they were also dangerous, even to their owners. "You people get hurt all the time, killed even," I reprimanded him. "So when you want to pet a pussy cat, when you want to touch and feel and stroke, it's my animals you come visit!"

It was probably only coincidence that at the end of that very day the arena trainer stumbled on a scene that demonstrated the difference between his animals and ours. Eager to help us load up for the next city, Ian Garden's men took over the teardown and packing of all equipment right after our last appearance. We weren't used to having this kind of help and in the confusion the cage holding Herk was inadvertently left parked in the way of the guy lines for the next act. Joy tried to move him by herself, made a little progress, and then decided she needed a robe over her thin costume. She returned in time to see Garden, in his emcee tuxedo, attempting to move the cage. "Don't touch that handle," she shouted, "it's a door," but she was too late. The cage flew open, leaving Garden staring right into Herk's nose. The tiger, seeing Joy approaching, knew he was in no danger. He simply went "Ffft-ffft-ffft," and sat down. Joy in turn walked up to the cage, said "Good boy, Herk!" and quickly closed the door. Garden was rattled to the core and for the rest of the tour he regaled anyone who would listen with the story of his near-miss. The arena man, having watched all this, quickly conceded that if the tiger had been one of his, Garden would not have lived to tell the tale.

4

A s with house pets, our animals come equipped with their own personalities, talents, and needs. The common element is the care and attention they all require—clean cages, a healthy diet, plenty of exercise. Hard as it is for 9-to-5ers to understand, we do have a full-time job.

When we first moved to Florida, in 1971, we felt safe and secure at the bottom of the St. Petersburg peninsula. At that time the area was crisscrossed by dirt roads and our only neighbor was blocks away, through a wilderness of palmetto, brush, and fallen pine trees. But in a rather short time houses began to spring up around us, the roads were paved, civilization intruded. As the decade drew to an end, we began to feel less secure and more harried. A couple of neighborhood kids took potshots at the kennels one night, with BB guns, after which we felt compelled to convert the oversized carriage house into a night kennel for the animals. People began to ring our doorbell at all hours asking if they could see the cats, or when the next rehearsal would be held. Some resourceful types found our telephone number, listed under our real names, and thought nothing of calling us to arrange a special show for a visiting in-law. We aren't antisocial, but like most people we do like our privacy.

The ranch near Gainesville solved all the problems we had had in St. Petersburg. It lies off the main avenues, far off, at the end of a very bumpy dirt road, and the house sits so far from the edge of the drive, shut off by a chain-link gate, that unexpected visitors have almost no chance of getting our attention. All around us are acres and acres of cattle and horse pasture, studded here and there by towering oaks. We can't see our nearest neighbor, and nobody can see our cats.

Our day starts as soon as the sun is fully up, because that's when our parrot begins his morning warm-up exercises. He is very quiet at first, as though testing the day. Hello. Hello? Hel*lo*? He gets a little louder until, when Joy hits the kitchen, he has risen to a screaming "HELLO!!!!!" While she gets the coffee going, the two of them engage in a top-of-voice exchange, simultaneously, with Joy squealing, "Pepe Taco! Hello! How ARE you? What a GOOD boy!" and Pepe running through his French and English right along with her, "Hello! Good boy! Aaauucckk! *Oui oui oui oui oui oui.* Hello!" At this point, I'm up. Nobody but the totally deaf could sleep through such a racket.

As soon as I have a little nourishment in me, I clean his cage, which usually resembles a small garbage dump from the orgy of the day before. At meal times, Pepe has to have some of whatever we're having. He doesn't want it to eat—he just takes what's offered as though granting us the privilege of sharing with him, and then drops it to the floor of his cage. Often amid the sunflower seed husks there will be a little spaghetti, bits of bread, half an apple, part of an ear of corn, a few nacho chips. And, of course, what does go into him at one end will inevitably come out the other—like the drive-through of a cheap Mexican restaurant. While I am cleaning up this mess, he wanders in aimless circles around the kitchen floor in a curious pigeon-toed waddle, muttering to himself or ex-

59

changing a few belly laughs with Joy. It's easy for her to laugh—I'm the one up to my elbows in parrot refuse.

Pepe's cage, now nicely clean, is set out on the screened porch so he can berate the dog whenever he wanders by, and Joy and I turn our attention to the cats. They are taken to their outdoor kennels and given fresh water, and then we clean and disinfect their nighttime cages and hose down the floor. Between a second cup of coffee and noon, everyone works out. We have a daily fitness routine of approximately three hours. Every other day we do exercises that include crunches (a sort of combined sit-up and leg-raise), chin-ups, pull-ups, and push-ups. Joy practices her splits and handstands every day, and also her disappearing act, an art that loses continuity and speed if she doesn't stay on top of it. On the days when we don't do routine exercises, we do ballet and adagio workouts. If the animals are not put through a complete rehearsal, they are at least run around the yard several times on long leads. Late in the morning Joy and I often jog, sometimes as far as six miles.

This fitness routine, combined with a rigidly enforced diet of low protein and high carbohydrates, has kept us trim and healthy for many, many years. It has kept our bodies young and strong and staved off the gradual disintegration of muscle that creeps up on everyone after the age of 30. If there were ever any doubts about whether it has all been worth the effort, the doctor who performed surgery on me in 1986 dispelled them. He could not believe the muscle tone he encountered, and the speed with which I recovered. So we stay with it. The only time the routine for man and beast is interrupted is when we are away from home on a job—the animals don't need to be rehearsed when they are working, and we usually can't find the time.

Afternoons are filled with chores. We have a large house with a big yard, and nobody takes care of it but us. In addition, costumes must be created, repaired or cleaned. Cages and props require the same treatment. The vehicles must be maintained and cleaned. There are frequent telephone calls concerning engagements, correspondence to be answered and books to be kept. If our days are filled, our evenings are quiet. Because we worry when we're away from our cats, we've sacrificed the kind of social life most people take for granted—a movie, dinner at a restaurant, a neighborhood party. We'd rather be at home where we can keep an eye on things. It seems that every time we cross our fingers and take a chance, the fates go out of their way to rap us across the knuckles. When a dear friend passed away in St. Petersburg, we decided it would be safe to make a one-day round trip from our ranch near Gainesville. Surely with the gate closed and the cats safe in their kennels, we wouldn't be missed for a few hours. When we got home, in the late afternoon, we found that fire ants had picked that day to tunnel under the chain link into Magic's cage. They had attacked the poor animal's tail, and he was in agony. The vet, summoned from the university, had to remove the better part of two joints from his tail and then we had to keep it tightly bandaged for weeks afterward to keep him from gnawing at the wound. Joy parked him on the kitchen floor in the magic cage and slept next to him every night for a couple of weeks, waking to dissuade him whenever she heard him chewing at the bandage. Now when people tease us about being reluctant to leave the house even for the supermarket, we can point to this incident. We're not paranoid: Something out there really is waiting for us to turn our backs!

Just keeping food on hand is a time-consuming chore. It costs a lot of money to feed four cats, so Joy is constantly scouring the countryside in search of a bargain in chicken necks (two hundreds pounds at a time) or chuck roast. Unfortunately, even when we find the bargains, we can't afford to keep too much on hand, for fear we'll be called away suddenly and return to find the area has suffered a power failure and our freezer is full of ... garbage.

Fortunately, Joy and I are always dieting. Although there have been times when the bank account was the de-

61

terminer of the contents of our refrigerator, for the most part what we eat is another aspect of our fitness program. Most people would probably find it very difficult to stick to the sort of regimen we've developed over the last 15-plus years, but it has served us very well. The main ingredients are cabbage, barley soup, pea soup, and garlic. Lots of garlic—a smelly but extremely healthful edible which I crush into cottage cheese and which Joy washes down like pills, with skim milk. Toast with a little low-fat cheese, a spoon of peanut butter, prunes, a hardboiled egg. If this sounds boring, consider Joy's philosophy: If you're sick and tired of the same thing day after day, you're bound to eat less of it. Except on Sunday. Sunday, when we aren't working, is pig-out day—the day when I can get into my cellophane bag of really awful junk food and Joy can have all the light beers her heart desires.

The diet, like the exercises, is difficult to follow when we're away from home. It isn't that we can't find the ingredients, or ways to prepare them. What happens is that in the time crunch of preparing for and performing two or three shows a day, something has to give. That something is food. As a result, we usually return from a road trip weighing less than when we started out, but also suffering from slightly diminished muscle tone because of the inability to follow our fitness routine.

In addition to keeping ourselves and our animals in good health, we are constantly improving the cats' quarters, working toward the habitat environment instead of the traditional, rectangular kennels. Water is a great source of delight, both for the animals and for us, watching them enjoy it. Demi will sit for hours curled up in his pool with his head sticking up at one end and his tail draped over the other. When the Florida summer strikes, even the palm leaves we hang over the kennels don't keep out the heat, and then Hercules will take advantage of the huge, galvanized tub in his kennel. Because he isn't "cool" like Demi, he can't just settle into the water and relax. He always has to use his great paws to knock the water around a bit and then send a tidal wave overboard when he crashes in.

The kennels are more than home to the cats. They are havens, places for retreat and privacy. An animal is as much entitled to his own space as is a person. This sense of space means that, in the afternoon, which is the cats' customary time for rest, if we aren't performing, we leave them alone. It also means that what goes through the chain link belongs to them. Because of the smaller kennels we built in St. Petersburg, the only pool was in Demi's cage. One particularly hot day we switched him to Hercules' kennel so the tiger could take a dip. At the end of the day, we couldn't get Herk out. He refused to budge and all the coaxing in the world was of no use. We finally realized the problem: His dinner dish was still in there with him. Until we retrieved it—I distracted him at one end while Joy fished the bowl out through the other with a broom handle—no power on earth would move that tiger.

When we first became keepers of wild animals, we made the same mistake a lot of people do with their pets—we thought it was cute to give them toys. We anthropomorphized, thinking of the animals as furry children who needed to be entertained and kept busy. Animals in the wild do not have toys; they don't even dream about toys. Professional trainers, seeing Hercules addicted to a rubber fried egg, told us not to put "foreign objects" in the cages. It was Demi who taught us once and for all that they were right. He literally ate everything we put in the cage, including a tire. Now, other than the tub for water and Demi's pool, the only "foreign objects" in the kennels are natural things like large tree stumps for scratching (or, in Herk's case, for knocking about) and raised platforms for the leopards, since in the wild they ordinarily climb into trees to sleep.

One of the rewarding things about raising animals with love and reward, instead of beating, punishing and using cruel stimulants, is that when we approach the kennels, we don't get roars and growls but purrs and that moist, sibilant "ffft, ffft" from Herk. This is the tiger's "howdy" to one of his own kind. It makes us swell with pride to know that this is the way he perceives us. The purring isn't saved just for us, either. For a while Magic had a crush on Herk, and would rub up and down along the chain link between their kennels making a throbbing noise like an outboard motor. For me the leopard has yet another call, his "I'm settling down for the night, Dad. Sleep well." It's a staccato roar that sounds exactly like someone sawing wood. He does it every evening.

It would be hard to say who, between the jaguar and the tiger, is better at being cute. Both of these big cats do things that make them seem at times like nothing more than overgrown kittens.

Had we known then what we know now about jaguars we never would have bought Demi, but no one warned us and certainly the man at the animal compound wasn't about to discourage us from taking the cat off his hands. Jaguars are without a doubt the most dangerous of the big cats. Very few acts use this animal—it is widely believed that they cannot be trained. Obviously this is a myth. What is no myth is that they do not give forewarnings of attacks. Demi is the only cat we have ever had who does not show signs of anger. Unlike the other cats, his eyes do not glow a golden color when he is enraged, nor do his ears go flat. He simply attacks. On the other hand, he also performs like a robot, doing the same thing in the same way night after night, more reliable than Old Faithful. Nothing fazes him. His memory is prodigious, both for people and places, and he never loses the little details he's been taught, unlike the other cats who will occasionally forget some tiny thing or throw in something that shouldn't be there.

There are other differences, too, between the jaguar and the Old World cats. Demi's coat does not thicken and thin with the weather, a trait which makes him more susceptible to cold than the others. By the same token, his fur always looks perfect because he is never betwixt and between one growth or another. He has often been de-

64

scribed as looking like a stuffed animal because physically he is flawless. Sitting absolutely still, he doesn't look real.

When Demi is feeling unusually content with the world, he does things that make us wonder how he could ever be called dangerous. He lies on his back, paws in the air, limp as a ragdoll, soaking up the sun. He curls up in a tight ball and sucks his toes. He rolls over and stands on his head, rear end in the air, the way babies sometimes sleep. When Joy gives him a bit of chuck roast for a treat, he insists upon sucking it dry before swallowing. A trancelike expression comes over his face, and then he turns his back while the juices run down his chin and Joy pleads, "Demetrius! *Swallow* that!" And he likes a good game. Joy can step up to the kennel, reach through the food slot, take a firm grip on his tail and pull as hard as she can, all the while singing, "We're . . . gonna . . . play . . . that . . . game . . . called . . . pullthejaguar'stail, pullthejaguar'stail." Demi will tolerate this indefinitely. But he is also rude to strangers. While the tiger and leopards will simply ignore someone they don't know, Demi will make a point of padding slowly to the far end of his kennel and turning his back.

Since we added Magic to our menagerie, Hercules is no longer the youngest, but, as Joy always says to our audiences, he truly is the "baby." If ever a cat was born to be a lover, it's our tiger. Except when he's crowded over his dinner dish, muttering under his breath to imaginary enemies who want to steal his food, he is the gentlest of creatures. I don't want to go so far as to say he's a coward, but he certainly isn't a fighter. I still laugh at the memory of a winter several years ago when we were touring the Midwest with a sports show. It was bitter cold, so cold that I had to exercise the cats indoors, by running them around the exhibits after the crowds had gone for the evening. The place was set up like a wagon wheel, with big exhibits in a center ring and smaller ones up the radiating side aisles. At the end of one of these stood an enormous stuffed grizzly bear, in *rampant* position, fully extended. Stretched out like that, it was at least six feet tall, not counting the base on which it stood. Puffing around the auditorium one night, with me in tow, Herk had a fancy to visit that aisle, and though I pulled and yanked and yelled "No!" he took off to explore. When that much tiger decides he wants to go *this* way, nothing will convince him to go *that* way. His reaction when the bear came into his line of vision was almost indescribable. In one motion he saw, absorbed, went "Ffft," turned on a dime and was heading back the way he came, almost trampling me in the process. He never broke his stride. It was all I could do to hang onto the leash because I was weak with laughter. The following evening, as we approached that area, he suddenly switched from my right side to my left, and stayed there until he felt we were safely away.

We can never forget that these are strong animals. With both their teeth and their claws they can inflict tremendous damage. Both of us have been injured several times. The slightest of these can be nothing more than bleeding spots on my arm where Magic's rough tongue has rubbed off the skin. (Imagine the feel of a house cat's tongue and then multiply that by a factor of ten or more.) The gravest of mishaps—well, more of that later. People often wonder how we feel about being wounded by our own cats. It happens. It's part of the lifestyle we have chosen, and we know that whatever happens, the animal is simply responding according to its instincts. While we can boast that all the major accidents have been the result of someone else's stupidity or ignorance, this statement doesn't say much for the public's awareness of the potential deadliness of wild animals. Time after time it has been proved that the animal needs protection from people, and not the other way around.

5

In the beginning, when we had only Aladdin and one guard dog, we drove around in a station wagon. When that vehicle was wrecked after being sideswiped by a semi in Georgia, we progressed to a step-van and trailer, which served us well for many years. But my dream was to have a trailer big enough to hold all of us together, including sleeping quarters for us separate from those of the animals. When we finally had enough money to do just that, I designed a fiberglas, 40-foot fifth wheel, hauled by a pickup truck with a huge engine. Christened the *Enterprise*, it contains a forward, raised compartment for us and our costumes, and a huge rear area for the cages, proper drainage, and, best of all, a battery-driven winch powerful enough to haul Herk and his cage up the ramp and into the trailer.

We must be a sight on the road, with my 100-pound wife at the wheel and me in the passenger seat sewing rhinestones on costumes. Other truckers honk and wave at us in disbelief and are thunderstruck at truckstops to see Joy step out of the cab. I often wonder what they would say if they knew she is technically blind in one eye! But that's the way we are: Joy likes to drive, and I like designing and making new costumes and repairing the old ones. Since we've been doing this unusual division of labor for almost two decades, I guess you could say we were among the first to do away with traditional husband-wife roles.

Joy mumbles a lot about how poorly she maneuvers the fifth wheel but the truth is that she has the stamina and endurance of an Army mule, and a lot of horse sense. She is our navigator, our bookkeeper, nurse and cook. She runs the house—and it's a big house—keeps me on an even keel when things go wrong, and still manages to look like something off a magazine cover. Well, except around the house, where she is prone to wearing outfits that make her resemble a character her mother calls "Maggie at the Pump"—a faded t-shirt and worn cut-offs. Planning is her forte, so when we set off on a long haul, she begins days in advance to arrange for the closing of the house, the buying and storing of extra food, and, most important, the route. One of the dangers of driving a rig as long as our fifth wheel is having to pull into places with no turn-around room. Most fast-food restaurants are off our list, as are many motels. Joy is extra careful about carrying an adequate supply of food because having to leave the expressway and go into a town to look for a supermarket can be very frightening.

On the whole, traveling around the country is enjoyable, if the vehicle holds up and the weather doesn't give us a hard time. There is, of course, the occasional boredom on the road. We had an assistant along with us on one long trip—all the way from Florida to Calgary—and one day when we were all bored to death with the passing wheat fields and telephone poles, I encouraged him to pull a little trick on Joy. She didn't know that for weeks Mark had been climbing into the cage with Venus. Now, tooling down the highway, I signaled him to do just that, then casually turned to Joy and said, "Hey, where did Mark disappear to?" She tried to look around while keeping the van and trailer on the road. "What do you mean, where is he? Where else could he be. . . . Oh, my God, you two are out of your *minds!*" For a very brief instant she thought we had come up with some new illusion. Perhaps Mark only *seemed* to be in the cage. But then, just as quickly, she realized it was no illusion. In a panic, she hit the brakes and nearly lost control of the van. To this day, when we remember that incident, I laugh and she glares at me.

Once at our destination, we carefully assess the circumstances of our appearance, especially where we fall in the schedule. Because we have to place our cats in tight positions for the illusions, we prefer to wait until the very last second before pre-setting them. When they're uncomfortable, we suffer with them. Over the years Joy has developed ways of quickly sizing up each show, learning exactly when to begin putting on her toeshoes and when to pre-set the animals. If the song that closes the act before us is, say, "Hooray for Hollywood," Joy will actually count the syllables. "Hooray for HOLlywood". . . pre-set Magic in the mirror ball. "Da da da da da da da DAH da da". . . put Demi in the magic cage. And so on. But if we follow an act that has a tendency to go into encores, and find that we have pre-set the cats too soon, Joy must be prepared to poke little pieces of meat through the traps into waiting mouths, to keep the animals content.

One saving grace is that we do not have to force Demi and Magic into position. Our cats do their bits quite voluntarily. It still amazes me to watch them climb into places that must run counter to their instincts. No pushing, no shoving, no begging, no pleading. The trap for Demi is opened, he steps into the cage and of his own accord moves into place, sits down, and waits for the trapdoor to be closed. There are probably not three extra inches in that compartment, in any direction, but he never complains.

I am so accustomed to dealing with my cats, and to expecting them to react in a certain way, that I occasionally forget that not everyone's animals are as cooperative as mine. In the Garden circus in Canada where we had so much trouble not too long ago, there was also a bear act. Circus people are famous for their willingness to pitch in and do double duty when they're not performing themselves, and the bear trainer needed someone to keep the animals quiet in their seats while he was running one of them through a motorcycle ride or dance routine or whatever. My job was to stand by and slip sugar cubes onto the long tongues they poked through their muzzles, and to make sure they stayed put. I was on duty one day during a performance when the "head" bear, a seven-foot brown monster named, of course, Bruno, suddenly pulled his muzzle off. Annoyed, I grabbed it out of his paw and said, "Bruno, you put that on right now!" And shoved it back over his nose and buckled it behind his head. "Sit down!" I was giving him a calming bit of sugar when I looked up and saw the trainer and his wife gaping at me, faces white as sheets, eyes popping out of their heads.

If I had been thinking clearly, I would have realized immediately the danger I was in, but I'm used to being firm with my cats, and with small children, and I had come to know these bears so well that I just plain forgot that they were . . . bears. When the act was over the trainer rushed up to me with an odd mixture of awe and bewilderment on his face. "The last guy who tried to put Bruno's muzzle on got bitten clean through his hand." My knees went rubbery.

Adventures, mishaps, accidents and near-misses we've had aplenty, but in all the years of traveling around with the cats, using cages and vehicles in various states of disrepair, we have "lost" a cat only once. I was loading the animals into their partitioned areas in the old step-van after a performance at the Barn Dinner Theatre in St. Louis. The parking lot just outside the dressingroom door was empty. Joy and the other members of the cast were inside, packing up, chatting, taking their time. The loading was a simple enough process, one I had done dozens of times, but I was in a hurry because it was bitter

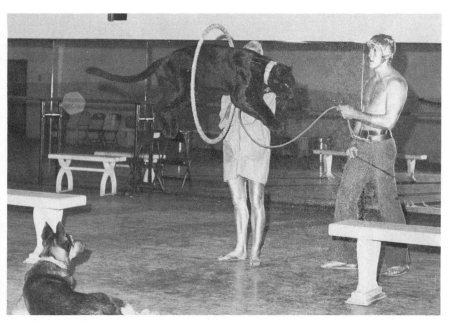

Still wearing our silver makeup, we rehearse Aladdin between performances at Radio City Music Hall as the leopard's companion, Diamond, looks on.

The "odd silver man and his black cat" taking the air atop Radio City Music Hall.

Aladdin in performance at the Americana Hotel in Miami in 1974.

Above: Demetrius at 12 weeks. His feet are an indication of what the jaguar will become when fully grown. *Below:* Now about a year old, he poses with Joy at the El San Juan Hotel in Puerto Rico. He still has big feet.

Growth of a tiger. Between 2 months *(top)* and 10 months *(bottom)*, Hercules conquered the kitchen.

Fully grown, Hercules is literally bigger than a refrigerator.

Demetrius demonstrates his sit-up during a backyard rehearsal. The markings on his underside are truly wonderful.

Opposite: Magic and I share a book during a break.

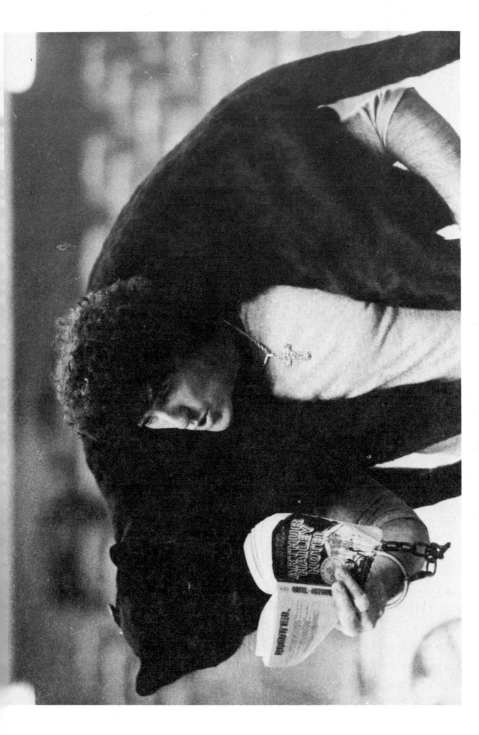

Who says tigers don't have a sense of humor!

Opposite: Adonis prepares to leap on command during a work-out in St. Petersburg. No whips, no prods — only my voice.

cold. Maybe my mind was wandering as well. Whatever the reason, I neglected to close the back door before putting Demi in from the front and in a flash he was standing on the edge of the van, the tip of his tail twitching in delighted anticipation. Before I could even gasp in surprise he was on the ground. It was dark. There was a moon, and lights in the parking lot, but not far away there was a stand of trees, and beyond that . . . who knows? A light snow had fallen and for several seconds Demi danced around in surprise at this new sensation under his feet, leaping and sliding in circles, making swirling paw prints. Great billows of cloud-breath belched from his nostrils so that in the moonlight he looked like a spotted dragon. He was having a marvelous time while I stood frozen in my tracks, my heart beating furiously.

Before I could move toward him, Demi leaped up on a Cadillac illegally parked by the stage door. I managed to grab his tail but couldn't hold it, and he pulled away from me, in his excitement knocking flat the car's radio antenna. At this point I got a grip on myself, marched over to the van, flung wide the door and said, "Demetrius! Get back in there right now!" To my utter astonishment, he did as ordered.

Unbelievably, through what seemed like an eternity but was probably only a minute or two, no one stepped through the stage door. Expecting company at any second, I quickly seized a nearby broom and swept away the paw prints so there would be no signs of Demi's escape, and then, I'm ashamed to admit, I leaned a ladder over the fender of the Cadillac. The owner was one of the first people out of the building and I hid in a cowardly fashion in the van listening to her bemoan that a falling ladder had smashed her antenna. You had no business parking there in the first place, I muttered to myself guiltily.

I was so embarrassed about the whole affair that I didn't tell Joy until about three weeks later. I expected a firm lecture on the subjects of laxity, stupidity, sloppiness, neglect, and the like, but she just turned a funny color and looked like she was going to lose her lunch.

71

PART
3
On the Road

1

While it is safe to say that the up-and-down quality of our lives began in earnest the day we took on the care and feeding of a wild animal, a great deal of water had already gone over the dam long before Aladdin came on the scene. Unless you're a superstar, with a veritable army of underlings taking care of your every whim, you run into problems, take risks, make bad choices, and often wind up with egg on your face.

In 1962, when we were just getting established as an adagio duo, we were put under the wing of an agent named Fred Harris, who was more or less typical of the patient, hardworking, behind-the-scenes types who boosted our careers along. Fred put up with a lot from us. His taking us on in the first place is a tribute to his fortitude. The first time we performed for him we were "doubling," an exhausting routine that involves performing in the first show at one club, then dashing across town to appear in the late show of another. At the first show, with Fred watching from the wings to see if he wanted to add us to his stable of nightclub performers, a ribbon broke on Joy's toeshoe. It unraveled and unraveled and unraveled until it was flapping in all directions, including in my face. Fred just waved it all away as we apologized profusely. We promised Fred that the next performance would be flawless.

We made a mistake at the second hotel we have never made since. Joy did not peek out to check the stage before she made her entrance. She had no way of knowing that the MC had left a microphone in her path. She was wearing a skirt made up of strips of material that whirled around her, and as she pirouetted gracefully out before the audience she spotted and evaded the microphone but her skirt didn't. First the strips entwined themselves around the stand. Then the stand fell to the floor, throwing the microphone itself into the air so that the wire snapped up and wrapped itself around Joy's neck. She was literally being mugged by an inanimate object. If we had wanted a comedy routine, this would have been unbeatable. She managed to extricate herself and kick the gadget out of her way as I danced on stage to join her, but for a few seconds she looked ridiculous beyond our wildest nightmares. Once again, Fred understood. He had been half of a dance team at one time and had probably been through similar adventures. "We like to see how you work under pressure," he said.

In the fall, despite our talent for making fools of ourselves, another manager, Buddy Morra, helped arrange our first European tour. We flew over with money saved from our many club dates and the trip was uneventful, despite Joy's insistence on taking along our poodle, Paillette, hidden under a pile of beige yarn in a straw basket. As an extra precaution against the prying eyes of customs officials, she layered the top of the basket with a few items of peculiarly female hygiene. We successfully smuggled the dog with us through three countries, although there were moments when we had to rely heavily on the poodle's innate intelligence and good training. One day a chambermaid, dusting under our eyes in a hotel room, lifted poodle and basket off the coffee table.

Instantly we broke into an animated and ad-lib conversation about our travels, during which Joy enunciated ever so clearly, "So, anyway, I think we really ought to STAAAAY around a few days." Paillette staaayed.

We had cabled ahead to our first stop, London, to reserve rooms at the site of our appearance, the Savoy. It never occurred to us to book under anything but our real names, Mr. and Mrs. Ronald Guay. We checked in, unpacked, rested awhile and then, with coats thrown over our leotards, rode downstairs to survey the stage and general working conditions. We greeted the stage manager and introduced ourselves and were in the middle of a discussion about lighting and music when a bellboy appeared and wordlessly set our luggage at our feet, all repacked. Behind him came the manager, who informed us with a nose aimed somewhere over my left ear that artists were not permitted to stay at the hotel. Management had not realized that the Ronald Guays were Ron and Joy Holiday or they never would have booked us in the first place. Insult was added to injury when we were left to our own devices to move our bags and baggage across the street to the Strand Palace, a perfectly acceptable hotel but nowhere near the luxury of the Savoy. The whole affair was distasteful in the extreme and left us feeling like dirty American cousins.

Although it was August, London was cold, and the audiences were as chilly as the weather. We probably would have been big hits in the music halls, with their variety acts and audiences of the "people," but the upper-crust clientele at the Savoy sat like wooden dummies through most of our performances. After two weeks we were delighted to board the boat train for France to spend some time with friends before moving on to Italy.

We got to Rome without further incident, to perform at the Casino della Rose, a lovely place set in the middle of a park filled with trees and bushes. The performances were *al fresco*, which made a lovely setting for our adagio.

The owner of the Casino della Rose was our first contact with what might be generically called The Mob. His money-making scheme consisted of canceling out an act after one week, on whatever grounds he could invent, bringing in someone less expensive, and pocketing the difference. We were warned about this practice by Christian Ygrouchki, a wonderful Cossack dancer at the Casino. "He'll offer you a booking at another place he owns in a different city," he predicted, "and it's not a bad place. Don't cross him. He can be a very dangerous man."

Events transpired exactly as Ygrouchki foresaw, but I refused the owner's offer. Young, arrogant, and probably thoroughly out of touch with the situation, I told him that two weeks was our minimum stay in any one place because traveling is so exhausting. When he dug in his heels, I placed a call to Buddy, who advised me to hold my ground and to inform the owner that if he persisted in treating his performers this way he wouldn't get any more acts from the States. This threat didn't go down very well but for the time being at least we seemed to have a victory.

It was near the end of our two-week appearance that I learned how the casino owner planned to recoup his losses. His girlfriend, frightened but determined to warn us, let on that he planned to have a couple of his friends "mug" us in the park on pay day.

We were all paid, in cash, on the night before the final performance. I knew we would never make it through the dimly lit park with our money, but I came up with a way to foil any muggers. As the cast mingled around after being paid, I raised my voice and said, "Everyone, listen! You've been such a great group, we want to thank you. You're all invited to be our guests at dinner tonight." There were cheers and whoops and girls fell all over me, planting kisses on my face, and then we strolled out into the park, firmly flanked by a mass of people who provided unwitting protection as we walked to a restaurant we freqented around the corner from our pensione. Four well-dressed men did indeed appear at the restaurant as our crowd began to settle in, but in the the noise and confusion I got Joy aside and handed her the camera case in which I had stuffed our thousands.

"Take this around to our room," I told her, "and hide it well."

Whether because of the humorless clerk who guarded our pensione or because of our barking poodle, no one broke into our room that night, and in the morning we were waiting at the doors of the bank across the street. Eight hundred dollars in lire looks like eight million, and when I dumped the money out on the counter to ask for a check to be sent to our bank in the States, there was pandemonium. Guards rushed to close and lock the doors, and for a moment we thought our adversary had sprung a trap. We were about to panic when someone explained that the street urchins make a practice of dashing into banks and snatching any money left within their grasp. As soon as our cash was safely under lock and key, the bank doors opened again and we strolled out into the sunshine.

From Rome we moved on to Campione d'Italia, on the Swiss-Italian border, performing at the Casino de Campione. The audiences here rivaled those at the Savoy for unresponsiveness. They consisted largely of well-heeled Milanese, many of whom were brought to the Casino via helicopter. They were not impressed with us. It was a great relief when, from time to time, a crowd of French or American or German tourists filled the Casino, because those audiences really appreciated us.

We were supposed to go from Italy to Barcelona and then on to Finland, but as we went to bed the night before our last performance at the Casino Joy had one of her "feelings." "I don't feel right about Barcelona," she said, and we agreed to reconsider the next day. The morning papers were filled with stories of terrible floods right in the neighborhood of Barcelona where we were scheduled to perform. In fact, the nightclub had been virtually destroyed. Having nowhere to go and unwilling to hang about for two weeks to do only Finland, we canceled the rest of the tour and prepared to sail home on the *France*.

Three years before, when Joy and I had returned home from our studies in Paris aboard the *America*, it had seemed obvious to us that, if we could make the right connections, we could exchange an appearance or two for a better cabin. Slipping through the unlocked gate one evening, in our best clothes, we had invaded the first-class ballroom and danced like mad fools in an effort to catch the purser's eye. The plan called for him to say, "Aren't you wonderful? Won't you dance for us in return for a first-class cabin?" Dream on. He threw us out. He got punished though. The seas on that trip were so bad that absolutely everyone on the ship was sick all the time, except me. I had the dining room to myself and ate like a trencherman all the way across.

Now, on the *France*, we resolved to try again. This was a special crossing. The ship was brand spanking new and outfitted with the most fabulous decor, including a white baby grand that rose up through the floor of the lovely little theater. Whatever the reason, this time we were able to pull it off, dancing for the captain's dinner and for shows in the first-class ballroom, in exchange for a luxury cabin. The captain was so taken with Joy that, upon being introduced to her, he kissed her hand and offered to slow down the ship during our performance so she wouldn't "turn her pretty little ankle." He wasn't joking, either. Balance is half our act and there's nothing worse than being in a precarious attitude on a listing ship. The seas were so rough that people in the audience were taking bets on whether or not Joy would fall from the toe stand. She never did.

Two years later we were back in Europe again, doing a tour that started in Germany, returned us briefly to the Campione d'Italia, on to Bern, and then climaxed with one of the highlights of our lives, a performance in Monte Carlo before Prince Ranier and Princess Grace.

In *très chic* Monte Carlo we got another dose of treatment as second-class citizens. The rich, the very rich and the excessively rich seemed determined to confine entertainers to the back rooms, out of sight except when on the stage. In the coffee shop at the casino we were stared at like freaks because we dared to walk in between shows, still wearing our stage makeup. At the Sporting d'Été, the open-air supperclub where we worked, we were barred from the clientele's restrooms. The performers' bathrooms, backstage, were so filthy that Joy refused to comply. She put on her chinchilla jacket and marched to the main lobby, where she was stopped and told the ladies' room was off limits. Here her French came in handy. "Hey!" she spat. "The day I come in here wearing jeans and looking like a slob, fine, throw me out! But I'm properly dressed and I'm going to use this bathroom and you can't stop me." And she walked on by.

Our appearance at the Sporting d'Été, for the annual Red Cross Ball, was at the behest of Princess Grace, who thought it would be nice to have an American team to remind her of home. The Red Cross Ball was a one-night gala attended by absolutely everyone who was anybody in Monte Carlo. The cast could talk of nothing but the royal family. We all knew that the Rainiers were out there and we kept peeking through the curtains or trying to perform with one eye on the audience in the hope of catching a glimpse of them. This was the second and last time in Joy's career that the pre-performance jitters failed to disappear, and she went through our entire adagio with a case of terminal butterflies. It was while we were taking our bows that I suddenly saw Princess Grace. She was standing up, smiling broadly and applauding vigorously, and just as I recognized her, she took the rose from the centerpiece on her table and threw it on the stage. I was flabbergasted; this is a gesture usually reserved for theater and opera. Others in the crowd followed suit, and soon the air was filled with flying roses, but I kept my eye on that first one and as we dashed off the stage I grabbed it. We still have it, pressed and framed under glass, a treasured memento of the fairy-tale princess.

2

At the end of the 1960s, our club dates were falling off, and Radio City was entering the first of its financial death throes, when our manager came up with an offer to appear for two months in a magic show in Mexico City. We sighed, checked the bank balance, and said we'd do it. Working outside the States can be frustrating and exhausting—but the handwriting was on the wall: Take the money while it's there.

The *Circo Magico Tihany* ran for five weeks in Mexico's capital, at the end of which Tihany asked us to go on tour with him as the star attractions. This time we had no misgivings about saying yes, because contrary to our fears of mud shows in lousy places with rotten food and poor living conditions, Tihany's circus had turned out to be first class all the way, and Tihany himself was the most straightforward, honest man we ever dealt with. "I don't believe in contracts," he told us as we discussed the tour. "A handshake will suffice." And it did.

Early in the tour, in the town of Morelia, I was walking Paillette behind our hotel one evening when the dog began sniffing and barking in a dark corner. I approached with caution, having great respect for the odd and unfamiliar reptiles of the lower Americas, but when I got close I saw that he had found a small child, perhaps four or five years old, huddled on the ground. He was wearing only rags, his stomach was severely distended, and he was foaming at the mouth. For a few seconds I was too shocked to move, but then I gingerly picked him up, trying to avoid the smells of urine and vomit, and bellowed for Joy to come down from our room.

The events that followed this apparently simple rescue mission were so traumatic that to this day I have trouble talking about the whole incident. Perhaps it's best if Joy explains. . . .

* * *

When I came tearing downstairs to see what Ron was yelling about, I couldn't believe my eyes. We stood there for a few seconds, like a couple of dummies, staring at this *thing*, totally at sea about what to do. Here we were, in a strange country, with only the slimmest idea of the local customs. Somebody had to do *something*. What kind of a place lets children die in the streets?

I left Ron standing there, sort of gibbering and jabbering over the child's wretched body, and ran inside to get help from the hotel manager, who sent us down the street to the police station. The overweight slob of a policeman on duty that night was anything but helpful. He could hardly be bothered pulling his feet off the desk to see what we were ranting about. "You Americans," he growled, "you get so emotional about everything. What have you got there?" Ron laid the child on the table but quickly picked him up again as the officer raised one foot with the intention of booting him onto the floor.

In the arguing that followed, I did my best to wring some meaningful advice from that man, who kept saying, "Put him back where you found him—if he lives to be ten, the military will pick him up." And I kept saying, "We can't do that." Finally, Ron lost his temper. "How can you sit under those pictures of Christ and the Virgin and call yourself a Christian?" he shouted at him. "You pig!" Knowing that nothing in the world will calm Ron down once he gets enraged like that, and seeing that the authority was turning a dangerous shade of red, I took Ron's sleeve and steered him out of the building. The "pig" shouted after us that a day or two in the local jail might change Ron's mind.

We turned to Tihany for assistance. Wise in the ways of Mexico, he first warned us that we were wading into very treacherous waters, and then steered us to the American hospital. On our way there Ron removed the tight belt around the child's waist. It had probably once held up a pair of pants but it was now cutting into his skin so deeply that he was bleeding. It was then that we noticed the egg-sized swelling on the end of his penis. If this little boy lived, he was in danger of being permanently disfigured.

The "American" hospital turned out to be run by Mexicans for wealthy foreigners. As soon as the doctors recognized the child as Indian, their mild disinterest switched to disgust. "He's from a tribe that lives in the caves about the town," one of them said, shrinking away from the boy as though poverty were contagious. Nobody would touch him until Ron began raising a stink again, and then a doctor reluctantly agreed to treat him if we put up $500 American. Tihany loaned us the money without hesitation.

Somehow, despite the constant vomiting, the malnutrition, and a dozen different infections, the child survived. We named him Juan Manuel—I don't remember why, the name just seemed to fit him. For two weeks I felt compelled to spend every free minute at his bedside, between shows. The schedule exhausted me, but I guess I felt the same sort of commitment that sets in now when we adopt a very young animal. Once a person takes on the responsibility of seeing a helpless creature through to healthy maturity, there can be no turning back just because the going gets rough.

The boy did not speak Spanish but an Indian dialect that was totally foreign to us. He was practically a savage, but he took to me instantly—he seemed fascinated by my blond hair. Over time we learned that he was a member of the Tarasco tribe, that his mother had gone away, leaving him in the care of grandparents. Not too many weeks before we found him his grandmother had died and then his grandfather as well. Alone and bewildered, Juan Manuel had wandered down from the hills seeking food in the town, where he had been treated like a rabid dog.

The show moved on to the next city, and we took Juan Manuel with us. What to do with him? Ron had made up his mind at a very tender age never to father a child. It seemed to him that most people make a hash of child-rearing, that the responsibility is so great and the odds against doing right are so poor, it just didn't seem worth the pain. For me, the ballet and the animals had always been enough. But this little Indian boy was a *fait accompli*; he was here and he needed love and attention. I found myself becoming increasingly attached to him. In the end, adoption seemed the only thing to do.

We found a lawyer to begin the mountains of paperwork required to adopt a child nobody wanted. It was a costly and lengthy exercise in bureaucracy, with forms and documents far out of proportion to the problem. The Mexican lawyer apparently saw a golden opportunity to take advantage of a couple of sentimental gringoes and kept raising his fees until Ron finally made it clear that we had forked over all we intended to pay.

Turning Juan Manuel into a civilized human being was a round-the-clock effort. It took us weeks to teach him not to urinate in the corners of the hotel rooms, and even longer to get him into shoes, which he resisted strenuously. Everything we did, everywhere we went was a new experience for him, and it was wonderful to watch him grow and thrive. I got an enormous kick when he stumbled onto new things, like the chocolate milk that a cast member brought back one day from a quick trip into Texas. He drank it like he was having a religious experience. And the fun I had shopping for clothes for him! All sorts of maternal tendencies I never knew I had began to seep to the surface. As the tour swung into its last leg, we took on a new lawyer to pick up the threads of the adoption effort. Even greedier than the first, this man, having been paid once, tried to extort an additional $1500 out of us, but we refused to pay him. He turned quite ugly, threatening us with arrest and, when that failed to produce the desired effect, offering to send a couple of "friends" to show us the light. In fact, on the last night in that town, two very hostile-looking men built like tanks approached the main tent, but the other members of the cast quickly formed a human chain around us and drove the heavies off. That was the last time anyone tried to bleed us for Juan Manuel's adoption, and a few days later we got the papers that made him legally ours.

By the time we reached the last few cities on the tour, Juan Manuel was a different kid. He had given in to shoes, minded his manners, learned to communicate. We had even had his teeth fixed, spending a hefty part of our earnings to undo years of neglect. He proved to be a sturdy little boy, stoical about pain, even to enduring the dentist's chair without anesthetic or a whimper. The only time he ever cried was when we banished him from our performance one night as punishment for having assaulted another little boy with a water pistol—filled with urine.

Punishment was rarely the answer to Juan Manuel's deviations from "civilized" behavior, such as when we discovered that he was stealing Paillette's food at night. We were giving the poodle adequate quantities of chicken in the absence of standard dog food, but suddenly he turned into a complainer, begging constantly for food. Once the thefts were discovered, we gave Juan Manuel the sole responsibility of going to the market for the chicken and giving it to the dog. He was extremely proud of this guardianship and took it very seriously. We began to suspect that our theories about child-rearing, created of course in that easy vacuum of remote observation, were really very good.

85

The tour was drawing to an end when we learned we were wanted for Radio City again. Our contract allowed for such things, and Tihany was gracious about accepting our withdrawal. On our last night he presented us with our final check, airfare to Mexico City, and his best wishes.

The trip to Mexico City was filled with excitement. It was Juan Manuel's first plane ride and he was simultaneously thrilled and scared to death; he prayed a lot. We in turn couldn't wait to introduce him to our home, to our friends and families. I had been writing letters telling everyone we knew about our new son and already parties were being planned in his honor, including a tremendous bash at Radio City.

But as we prepared to board the flight to the States, everything fell apart. The Mexican authorities, checking over our papers, informed us rather casually that the laws had changed. People adopting Mexican children could no longer bring them across the border. The new statute was designed to prevent quick and easy adoptions and in spirit it didn't apply to us, since we certainly hadn't gone to Mexico for that purpose. No matter. If we wanted to keep our son, we would have to stay in Mexico with him, forever.

Numb with fear, we appealed to higher authorities at the airport, only to hear the echoes of Morelia: "Put him back where you found him." In desperation, I did something totally uncharacteristic—I tried a bribe. I got down on my knees, literally, before one official and offered him my savings account passbook. "Please," I begged, fighting back the tears, "everything in this account is yours if you'll help us." His answer was, "You could get ten years for that, lady." I couldn't believe anyone could be so hard-hearted.

We postponed our flight and ran around helplessly for a couple of days, trying to find someone who could cut through the red tape that was strangling us. Our memories of who we saw and where we went are vague because we have spent a lot of time trying to forget. I have only the dimmest recollection of the hours we spent trying to make someone understand what the system was doing to us. Ron says it was a policeman with a slightly more humane nature than most who finally suggested a Catholic convent near Mexico City. The mother superior agreed to take Juan Manuel, but she pulled Ron aside while I sat in the car. I was crying so hard that I couldn't talk or even move. "You must promise," she warned him, "never to try to see or contact this boy. It wouldn't be fair to him to be pulled back and forth between your world and ours." Juan Manuel stood quietly by the door, his suitcases at his feet, his favorite toy airplane under his arm, patting Paillette on the head and telling him he would never see him again. Ron kept a grip on himself at the moment of parting, but I know he cried later, in his own private way, and that he burned all the pictures we had of our almost-son, secreting only one away until the day comes, if ever, when he can look at it without falling apart.

Every now and then, when that awful scene at the convent door creeps up and catches my memory by surprise, I relive the whole bad dream. Time, and my unshakable faith in a Supreme Being who moves with a purpose, have softened the pain for me, but the subject still drives Ron into a melancholy and uncharacteristic silence.

* * *

Our return to the States was dismal in the extreme. With Joy unable to talk about Juan Manuel and what went wrong, the burden of explaining to everyone that the parties were off fell to me. Having a little time to kill before we were needed at Radio City, we retreated to Maine to lick our wounds. Joy was so depressed that I went to see her family doctor, a wise and practical man who had cured her childhood rheumatic fever with such ingenuity that not a trace of the disease can be found today. He told me to get her back to work—fast. We left at once for Radio City, where Bettina Rosay took one look at Joy, asked hesitantly if everything was all right, and was astonished when Joy burst into tears. We began preparing for the show, but Joy remained shocked and wooden, doing her work in that stubborn, persistent, "show-must-go-on" way of hers, but without any heart at all. She was like an automaton.

That wasn't the last of it, either. Returning from rehearsals in New York one evening, we were approached by a neighbor who told us that two men from the F.B.I. had been ringing doorbells on the block asking whether we were "harboring a small, dark child." Those sons of bitches had nothing else to do but try to prove that we had found some way to smuggle Juan Manuel into the country. For a few days I was murderous.

About ten years later, we did hear from someone who had traveled through the area that Juan Manuel had grown into a fine young man and was working at the convent as a carpenter. We consoled ourselves then, and to this day, by remembering the wretched mess I had found on a dark street compared to the neatly dressed, well mannered, healthy little boy we left behind. It is some consolation, but not much.

3

$\mathbf{O}$ur first major engagement as an animal act was with the Hamid-Morton circus, which began its tour in March 1972 in Wichita, Kansas. It was not an auspicious start. With Aladdin in his cage in the rear of the station wagon, and Diamond on the back seat, we set out from St. Petersburg. We didn't get far. Near Valdosta, just over the Georgia state line, we were sideswiped by a semi, who paid no heed to the carnage behind him but drove off, leaving the wagon and the trailer twisted around each other in a ditch by the side of the interstate.

It looked a lot worse than it was. Perhaps the animal cage added reinforcement to the wagon. The doors of the trailer sprang open, scattering our equipment and papers in all directions. The rescue squad that arrived to cut us out of the wagon was mercifully halted by an alert fireman, who heard the gas tanks stored in the trailer hissing beneath our car.

Once free we checked each other out for damage. The force of the crash had blown open the refrigerator in the trailer, spewing eggs into Joy's shoes stored nearby. We were both shaken up, and my wig was a bit askew, but otherwise we were all right. Released from the wreck and held tightly on their leads, the two animals were not happy. Diamond became super protective, unwilling to let anyone near us, and Aladdin reverted to some savage state that left him snarling and hissing and suffering diarrhea in a circle around us.

One kind truck driver did have the courage to stop and ask if he could help, and Joy sent him dashing about the highway trying to rescue the pages of our address book that were flapping everywhere. Once the fear subsided, we got short-tempered, angry at the careless semi driver who had caused the mess and at the passing motorists who ignored our plight.

Eventually someone got me to a truck rental in Valdosta, where I was unfortunately put at the wheel of a vehicle with standard transmission. Years before, Joy had taught me how to drive one of these contraptions but I had practically gone out of my way to forget her lessons. The man on duty watched me with considerable doubt on his face as I hiccuped and kangerooed around the parking lot. "Yo' gonna kill yo'self," he ventured. I figured if I could survive being run off the road at 50 miles per hour, I could manage a bucking truck.

It seemed to take forever to retrieve whatever we could from the wagon and trailer, pack it in the rental truck, ease the animals into the cage, and get back on the road. The ride to St. Petersburg was a misery. We were black and blue, our props were damaged, and the highly attractive tour with Hamid seemed certain to be dead. Our nerves were so strung out that when the police came knocking on our door, not an hour after we crawled into the driveway, we expected all kinds of trouble. But they were only doing their job. Seeing a rented truck in the driveway, and knowing we were away, they thought burglars had taken over. They gave us a fright, but then we probably scared them, too. We must have looked awful.

We managed to track down Hamid in Atlantic City and tell him about the accident. He was not easily dissuaded.

"Are you all right?" he asked first. "Are the animals all right?" And "Can you put your props back together?" Given affirmative answers, he said with authority, "Get back on the road. Buy another vehicle right away and meet the show in Kansas City." He was right. There was nothing to be gained by sitting around nursing our wounds.

We found the best vehicle we could in such haste, a Maxivan. It was spacious enough, but the overhead clearance in the loading doors required us to partially dismantle the cage, load Aladdin, and then reassemble. For the time being, it had to do.

Our families and old friends we hadn't heard from in years back in Maine learned of our plight, and as we arrived in the various cities of the Hamid tour we found money waiting for us. People seemed to know that we weren't in a position to purchase a new rig on such short notice and they contributed what they could. They all said we didn't have to pay them back but we did, every penny.

It was cold, very cold in Kansas City but we were given special permission, because of our animals, to pull the van into the auditorium. The advantages of parking indoors were quickly negated by the opportunity it provided for someone to break a window in the van and steal our African gray parrot, Polly. She had been given to me by a relative who had found her unwilling to tolerate the pokings and proddings of his children, and we were crazy about her. She had a genuine sense of humor: She would pull off my wig whenever I bent over near her perch, and she would sing duets with Joy, stopping exactly when Joy stopped, starting precisely with her again, never missing a note or singing an extra one.

When I discovered the burglary, I went berserk and tore around the lower regions of the auditorium looking into cars and searching everywhere in the dim hope that she was still around. I knew she didn't have much chance of survival. Most people have no idea what kind of care a tropical bird requires. Joy, meanwhile, was being given the news by one of the meanest men we have ever worked with. The son of a wealthy newspaperman, Paul was so unlovable that his father actually gave him the money to buy whatever animals struck his fancy and then paid him to stay out of town. Paul walked up to Joy and said, "Have you been downstairs? I hear there's an animal loose."

For a second Joy panicked, until she remembered she had just seen Aladdin in his cage. Paul's wife, who was basically a nice person, snapped, "Shut up, Paul. She doesn't know anything about it."

"I don't care," the man whined. "He's down there carrying on like an animal." He was referring to me.

Joy raced down to the parking area, found out what had happened, and then walked up and down every aisle of the auditorium, looking behind and under every seat. The next day her legs were so sore she could hardly move. We were grief-stricken over the loss of Polly and still think about her and wonder what became of her.

New as we were to the animal-act business, we thought everyone who kept wild animals would have enough sense to realize that their livelihood depended on keeping their investments content and happy. It never occurred to us that there were people like Paul in the world. We ran afoul of him and his nasty disposition several times during the Hamid tour. We probably would have forgiven him his personalty traits had he not been such a demon with his animals. He had the best, of course, since he could afford to dispose of any creature who didn't please him and simply purchase another. The one we felt the sorriest for was Pumpkin, the hippo. Paul had dim ideas, founded on ignorance, about training her. As far as we know this cannot be done. His misguided efforts included depriving her of water when she didn't behave according to his expectations. Overhearing him tell his attendant not to give Pumpkin water one night because she had misbehaved, we waited until it was quiet in the auditorium and then we crept down to the level on which Pumpkin was housed, attached a hose, and watered her down. Oh, how she loved it.

The next morning we could hear Paul raving about somebody disobeying his orders. He probably suspected us, but all he could do was disconnect the faucet and thus avoid a repeat the following night. Undaunted, we filled buckets with water, carried them to the hippo, and wet her down. Shortly after we went to bed, we heard incredible crashing, smashing sounds coming from that level of the auditorium. We climbed out of the van and looked down onto the main floor to see Pumpkin having the time of her life. Somehow she had got loose and was having a ball running full tilt into the rows of folding chairs set up for the morning's audience. She was almost systematically leveling the place, knocking down light poles and anything else in her path. It never occurred to us to try to stop her.

Sometime during the next day Pumpkin vanished, only to be replaced in a few days by a gigantic male lion, Samson, who got loose one evening during a cast picnic and caused havoc for an hour until he was recaptured. Had the picnic not been held in an enclosed football field, Samson might yet be wandering the countryside.

Our troubles on this tour were not over. When the Hamid show closed in Kansas City, everyone had to be out of the building by two o'clock in the morning, but it was freezing outside and we had a van with a broken window that couldn't be repaired until early the next day. We were certain we would be given permission to lay over in the building but the answer was "Out!" We nearly froze that night. Covering Pepe Taco with every spare blanket and towel, we lay down on the floor of the van with Diamond between us for warmth. In the morning even Aladdin's urine was frozen.

4

Our first big hotel appearance was at the Americana, in Bal Harbour, near Miami. The show, *Femmes Fatales*, was held in the Bal Masque supperclub and also featured a trio of very funny comedians, as well as a juggler. We were working hard but enjoying every minute of it when we had another "accident" with Aladdin, this one of more serious proportions. The juggler employed his wife as an assistant; her job was to stand to one side and toss the objects—pins, balls, whatever—to him as he juggled. What happened was really no one's fault. Before each performance, as we came down the hall toward the stage with Aladdin on the leash, we always called out loudly, "Clear the hall, here comes Aladdin," and the dressingroom occupants hastily closed their doors and stayed out of the way. The juggler's wife had just flushed a toilet one evening and didn't hear us coming. She stepped out of her room as we passed, landing flat on Aladdin's foot. It was a chance timing that could never be repeated. Aladdin bit her on the calf.

It wasn't much of a wound. Aladdin's defanged mouth wasn't capable of inflicting the sort of damage we saw later from the other leopards and the jaguar. And at first the juggler's wife seemed very cooperative and casual about the bite, assuring us she wouldn't even think of suing. We didn't discover until weeks later that she already knew we didn't have liability insurance when she made this generous statement. But toward the end of our eight-month engagement at the Americana, she filed suit against the hotel and the producers, suddenly announcing that the bite had ended her modeling career. Modeling career? It was the first anyone had heard of this new profession.

The juggler and his wife made four big mistakes with the lawsuit. Their first was replacing the wife immediately with a thoroughly untrained assistant, who performed perfectly, thus destroying any illusion that the wife was a vital part of the act. Second, the juggler bragged to me one evening that when the money from this suit came through he would be able to retire, and even ventured to wonder what sort of money he would get if he shoved his wife's other leg in the cat's mouth. Third, the wife came backstage each day on crutches, but when her toddler wandered away from her, she dropped them and ran after the child, showing the whole world just how much the crutches were needed. And fourth, but most important of all, they completely underestimated the power and determination of the producers of *Femmes Fatales*. These men were hardened business people; they were not pushovers. Just how concerned they were for the wife was demonstrated bluntly one day when they walked by her dressingroom as she sat with her wounded leg propped on a table. She expected them to stop and inquire about her health but they strode by without a glance, right into our room. We heard about this snub for days afterward.

Assuming we had heard the last of the juggler's wife and her lawsuit, we went on about our business, but peace and quiet were not on the menu. We were awakened one night by violent pounding on our motel-room door and cries of "Open up! Police!" Stumbling around in the unfamiliar darkness, we managed to get the door open, only to be shoved back as what appeared to be about a dozen uniforms burst into the room. We were rudely held against the wall by drawn guns and were at a complete loss to understand what was happening until we heard something about "harboring a black panther." Or, to be more precise, "harboring a Black Panther." We heard the nightly news; we knew what they were talking about. There was tremendous confusion for a few minutes until Joy was able to get their attention. "If you'll just *listen* for a second," she bellowed, "we can explain!" The police halted in their tracks. "We *do* have a black panther. . . . " The tensing of a dozen sets of muscles was almost audible. "He's out in the car. . . . " Several officers started for the door. "WAIT!" shrieked Joy. "He's an animal. . . . " That didn't help. "I mean, wait! There are dogs. . . . " The situation was degrading rapidly. Finally she hit the right note. "He's got *four legs*." That at least got attention.

At length we were able to lead the police to our van, hold them back while I got the dogs out of the way, and then, by the glare of flashlights, demonstrate the dark, furry object in the cage. There followed a series of muttered expletives and then a lot of red-faced police apologized, returned to their respective vehicles, and drove off.

It doesn't take much imagination to figure out how a story like that gets started. One person overhears "black panther," repeats a half-heard conversation until the news reaches someone with just enough paranoia to call the authorities—and voilà, mass confusion.

5

Early in 1975 we joined a circus tour that was hitting various cities in Texas. It was not a class act. Unlike the Tihany circus, with its comfortable conditions and generous atmosphere, this circus was a true "mud show," a main tent set up in an unpaved parking lot behind a shopping center. Rain arrived two days before opening, making rehearsals impossible.

During the very first performance, I went to put the collar on Adonis after he appeared in Joy's place in the "magic cage." Only a split second before, someone in the stands had thrown a rock, hitting Adonis in the middle of the forehead and gouging a wound that continued to re-open over and over for months afterward. I did not see the rock or even hear the impact, nor did Joy, who of course was in hiding following her disappearance. As soon as my arm came within reach, Adonis sank his teeth into it. Four full-grown fangs penetrated my arm, all the way through.

When Joy reappeared we put a hasty end to the performance and got off the stage. "We are not making the same mistake we made with Aladdin," Joy warned. "You *will* go to the hospital."

Still in our costumes, we dashed to the emergency room, where I was left lying on a gurney for hours while the young nurses giggled and tittered at my stage clothing. My left arm was hanging off the far side of the table, out of sight, so that no one noticed I was on the verge of bleeding to death. Finally someone took a look, announced that the bite wasn't too bad, bandaged it, and sent us back to the van.

In the morning my hand was the size of a balloon and hurt like fire. Back in the hospital I was told to wait, again. I must have been in pretty bad shape, because when a marvelous man, Dr. Rosen, arrived on the scene, he took one look at me and started yelling his head off, beginning with "Who is responsible for this?" Not only were the punctures very deep, not only was I weak from loss of blood, but infection was setting in at an alarming rate.

Dr. Rosen approached Joy, explaining that it was up to her to decide whether I should have an operation, which would remove a great deal of the flesh in my arm, or an amputation. Joy didn't hesitate. "Do you even have to ask that question?" she replied.

My arm was laid wide open, the infected flesh was removed, and we were told I would need about two weeks of care and observation in the hospital. Every morning the covering gauze was removed, a blood sample taken, and every afternoon I was told the infection, which was proving extremely tenacious, was still there.

Joy ran into immediate problems with the circus owner, who announced that our animals were too dangerous to be lingering around his circus and ordered her off the site. Sick with fear for me, facing freezing weather in an improperly heated van, with nowhere to go, she was literally thrown out into the cold. The owner said we had broken our contract, but in truth he had violated it from the first day when he failed to provide the electricity and water hookups required. He did give us a week's pay, twelve hundred dollars . . . in small bills! Joy never did figure out whether all the money was there.

Unwilling to attempt the long ride to Florida by herself, Joy somehow packed up the animals and equipment and took up temporary residence in the parking lot of the hospital, hoping for a change in either the weather or me, or both, that would alter her circumstances. It became obvious rather quickly that I was in for a long haul, and the weather refused to lift. In the end, she bid me a tearful farewell and set off to cover the 1200 miles alone. Lying in my bed thinking of her on the road with two cats and two dogs in that cold van, I nearly lost my mind.

Other patients joined me in the double room, got well, and left. I was becoming increasingly frustrated. After two weeks, with no expectation for a quick release, I began hoarding antibiotic capsules, taking only half of each dose and secreting the other half in the pocket of my jacket that hung in the closet. Taking a stroll one evening, wheeling my IV bottle along, I came upon the front door of the hospital. Like a convict, I planned my escape.

Joy made it to St. Petersburg. She called me every day and never let me know the hell she was going through at home trying to take care of the pets. The ride had been ghastly, chiefly because of the cold weather but also because, although Joy loves to drive, fear for me, anxiety about the animals, and boredom induced by having no one to talk to had produced a particularly exhausting trip. Prayer and a strong constitution had pulled her through.

With the help of a neighbor Joy was able to unload the van and get the pets into their respective cages. For a few days she tried to carry on by herself, exercising the cats, picking up after them and the dogs, feeding the menagerie, taking care of the house. It was typical of her that she was determined to take the weight of the world on her shoulders and not let me, or anyone else, know that it was crushing her. Her sister called and asked if she needed help; Joy assured her she could manage. But fatigue eventually took its toll. She set out jauntily from the back door one evening carrying the stainless steel dishes used to feed the cats and was halfway to the kennels before she realized that they were empty. The food was still in the refrigerator. She broke down and cried, and was still in a stew when her mother called. Mama, known affectionately as "the witch," had homed in on the vibes of trouble all the way up in Maine. "Mama," wailed Joy, "please come down. I need you." Two days later Mama was on the scene and some degree of normalcy was restored.

At the end of the fourth week I got up in the middle of the night, dressed, packed my few belongings in a small suitcase, slipped out the front door while the admitting nurse and guard were having coffee, and hitchhiked to the airport. Using a credit card, I booked a flight to Tampa and, during a two-hour layover in Atlanta, called Joy to let her know I was coming home. I didn't bore her with the details.

I made a bad mistake when I booked that flight: I checked my suitcase. Neatly folded inside was my jacket, in the pocket of which was my medication. What I didn't know when I absconded from the hospital is that I was being detoxified from the morphine. I may have felt all right, but I was in no condition to be flitting about the country. Sitting in the Atlanta airport waiting for my connecting flight, I suddenly became very ill. Chills, sweats, shakes—I was a mess. I managed to track down a stewardess, explained about the pills, and asked about retrieving my luggage. Nothing could be done, of course; the poor girl couldn't even tell which flight the bag was on. When she realized how faint I was, she steered me into a private office in the airport and called in a covey of four policemen who happened to be in the area.

The police took one look at me, recognized a drug problem, and were on the verge of arrest when the stewardess pointed out the plastic identification bracelet on my wrist. From that moment the men were a lot more solicitous and one of them even got on the plane with me and escorted me into Joy's arms in Tampa. I was so startled by this attentive treatment, and by the fact that no one ever asked me to pick up the airfare, that I later sent a letter to the Atlanta police department expressing thanks and appreciation. "No one," I pointed out, "ever talks about the nice things police do."

Once her mother had put things back on an even keel, Joy had devoted a great deal of time to developing the young jaguar's talents. After I had had a day's rest, she nervously offered to show me what she'd accomplished. As I watched, she hauled out the mirror ball, escorted Demi up on it, pointed the baton at him, and he sat up! It was his first trick. Joy was proud as a peacock, I was delighted, and Demi seemed quite pleased with himself. But the jaguar had forgotten me altogether. To this day I am only his servant, feeding him, cleaning up after him escorting him around on a leash. He is Joy's cat, her Sugar Bear. All because I spent four of what must have been very important weeks to him languishing in a hospital.

My arm was a mess. At least half the tissue had been removed and the skinny, atrophied thing that was left was all but useless. I went to work on it at once, exercising almost fanatically every day to build the muscles back to a point where at least an audience would not be able to notice that one arm was smaller than the other. Our first date was only two weeks away. The task seemed impossible.

Then came the moment when I had to put the leash on Adonis for the first time since he had tried to alter my anatomy. Gripping the ends of the collar in either hand, I worked my head and one shoulder into the cage . . . and froze. To say my hands were shaking is a gross understatement. Everything from my wrists to my fingertips was doing a samba, the chain on the collar rattling like sleighbells. I must have stayed there in a crouch for a full five minutes, with the sweat pouring into my eyes, while Adonis stared at me. A low, impatient noise in his throat seemed to be saying, "C'mon, will ya?" When I eventually summoned the courage to slip the collar around his neck, he made no movement or sound at all, as if nothing had ever happened.

By the time we were ready to leave for Ohio, for the Shriners' Aut Mori Grotto circus, the arm was considerably better but still obviously smaller than it should be. I made extra wide, leather wristbands to go with my "lion-tamer" outfits, and these completely disguised the problem. About halfway to Ohio a swelling like a big, purple egg suddenly appeared on my wrist. We had had the foresight to take along antibiotics and these at least allowed me to do the show without aggravating the infection. Ironically it was one of our first really big successes with the cats, but my grip wasn't what it should have been and on several occasions Joy had the feeling I was going to drop her. She must love me very much, because no one but a fool would let a man with a big purple wrist lift, drop and throw her around in front of a few thousand people.

The wrist remained swollen despite the antibiotics but I thought I had everyone fooled, until one day when I went into a bathroom, and the nurse who was on duty at the circus walked in behind me, right into the men's room. She caught me by the mirrors with my wristband off, grabbed the arm and said, "You better do something about that, you can't work with that arm." And left. I stood there for several minutes with my mouth open, wondering what unearthly pair of eyes had noticed what I had concealed so cleverly. Then I took a razor blade, gritted my teeth, and slashed open the purple egg. It was painful and revolting, but it worked. That was the last time the infection reared its ugly head.

* * *

The main concern after the Aut Mori circus was keeping Demi working so he could improve his repertoire, learn to tolerate all sorts of conditions, and not get fully grown before we had pumped into his head everything he could absorb. We were facing what appeared to be a long lull in our bookings when, driving along the main road in St. Petersburg one day, I spotted a place called the

102

"Stock Market" that advertised live entertainment. Actually, it was a "go-go" joint, with the concomitant drug and prostitution sidelines, but the manager was a pleasant woman who was intrigued by the idea of a dance-illusion act on her stage. I brought Joy in to check things out and she made notes that resulted in our modifying the adagio a bit to fit the small stage, and changing the disappearing illusion so that, instead of reappearing in the magic cage, Joy came strolling in the front door, which brought down the house. Actually, we really prefer to do the illusion that way but in most places the distance from the stage to the main entrance is so far that Joy would never make it. Most magicians rely on the use of a twin or double for this trick, but we had only Joy.

Joy was terrified of the place. She had visions of the rough clientele sneering and hissing at the adagio. Or worse, hurling beer glasses at us and the cats. Or shouting, "Take it off!" Nothing of the kind happened. Quite the reverse, the audiences loved us, and in the three weeks we were at the Stock Market we were treated royally. The eight or ten go-go dancers who worked there were truly nice people.

6

Later in the year, when we received an offer for what appeared to be an excellent opportunity, a tour with the Polack Cirkens in South America, we bid an emotional farewell to our friends at the Stock Market and prepared to leave the country, again. It wasn't our idea of a perfect arrangement. If travel in Mexico had been difficult, this trip was going to be especially hard, now that we were hauling around two large cats, their cages, two guard dogs, the magic props, as well as all the regular equipment and costumes. But we could scarcely feed ourselves and our pets on the income from places like the Stock Market, and the money offered for South America was good.

The circus, put together by a man we shall call Pedro, was part of a competition held annually in Lima in which circuses from all over the world perform for awards presented by the Peruvian government. While the honors are given to individual acts or performers, they bring glory to the circus which sponsors them, and thus redound to all the members of the troupe.

The contract called for first-class accommodations in Peru as well as for round-trip travel expenses. The difficult part was just getting to Peru. All our equipment and animals—Adonis, Demi and the two dogs—had to be flown by cargo plane, from Miami. What was worse, only one of us was allowed to go along as an attendant, leaving the other to fly by passenger line to Lima.

Pedro had told us to be dressed to the nines when we landed in Lima because there was going to be a big reception and all sorts of press waiting for us. There was certainly nothing happening when I landed with the cargo. There was no press, no welcoming committee, no Pedro, not even a truck for transportation to the site of the circus. Feeling let down, I asked a couple of airport attendants to watch the equipment and the animals while I went in search of the vet, warning them not to attempt to unload until I got back. They didn't listen, of course, and while I was away they tried to forklift Demi and his cage onto the ground. After a few misses, which left some nice dents in the cage, they finally got him up in the air, only to drop him, cage and all, on the ground. To this day Demi goes insane whenever he sees what Joy calls the "mean machine."

In the little customs office at the airport I woke up the official on duty and urged him to contact the vet so that I could get our animals approved for entry into the country. About three hours later, after the vet had appeared and done his job, a small, filthy, rickety truck, apparently provided by Pedro, arrived to transport me and my cargo to the arena. Since it was impossible to get everything into the truck at one time, I set about determining logical, safe combinations of animate and inanimate objects, at which point Joy arrived, all dolled up for the big reception in the mink coat we had bought during the height of our Radio City days, before we became sensitized to what a fur coat means to the original owner. There can be no more foolish feeling than arriving at a dusty, deserted airport dressed like a movie star to be greeted by one's own husband commandeering a vehicle out of *The Grapes of Wrath.*

We had been told by Pedro that his circus was being held in the Amauta, a large, covered arena perfect for these sorts of shows. Now the driver informed us that we would be at the Plaza de Acho, a bullfight arena. As we set about loading the truck for one of the six trips needed to get everything from the airport to the Plaza, I made a mental note to ask Pedro about this mysterious change in arrangements.

All in all, it was a tiring and very disappointing arrival. As soon as we were alone we considered turning right around and going home. Pedro had already broken so many clauses in our contract that we would have been perfectly justified in telling him just what he could do with his circus. But the logistics were staggering. The ordinary traveler, finding himself in a hostile environment, can simply pack up and catch the next flight out. We had hundreds of pounds of equipment, no way to transport it, and Pedro had our return fare. There was nothing to do but stick it out.

During our struggle to bring in and unload all the cargo, Pedro remained invisible. He didn't materialize until the last bit of equipment was off the truck, and then he gave us a glib story about being compelled to meet another act at the border. Asked point-blank why we weren't performing at the Amauta, he replied breezily, "Oh, if you'd known where you were performing, you wouldn't have agreed to come." Right he was.

The Plaza is a 200-year-old arena, the largest in South America. Pedro had created a circus atmosphere by covering it with a tent top, which was all very impressive. But our "first-class" quarters proved to be a tiny, airless room in the arena normally used to carve up the dead bulls. It was filthy and smelly and crawling with roaches. Pedro began to babble about putting a mattress on the floor so we could be with our animals, but we quickly made it clear that we wouldn't spend a single minute in that room, and neither would our pets. He blithely did an about-face and suggested we talk the arena manager out of his office; I suggested *he* talk to the arena manager. In the end we got the office and, after another struggle, a four-poster bed and a device to convert the room's cold water to hot. No sooner had we settled into our new quarters than Pedro and his wife walked in, looked around, and began making themselves comfortable. We wondered what they were up to until Pedro asked, "Aren't you going to leave while we shower?"

We looked at each other, both of us thinking, "The nerve of this guy." Joy said, "Pedro, you live around here. Surely you have a place of your own."

"Oh, yes," he replied, "but it isn't as nice as this."

"This" was about as close to a garbage dump as we'd care to get, but there was no way we were going to share it. We threw them out.

Lima is a dusty city. It sits on the edge of a desert to the Pacific side but, despite the mountains to the inland side, it never enjoys the rain. Everything is covered with dust, all the time. We never once saw the sun in Lima. Moreover, the Plaza is not in the most fashionable part of town, or even near the business district. Lima may be the largest city in Peru, and it may have many relics of the great Spanish center it once was, but, because our schedule and our cats restricted us almost completely to the area around the Plaza, we were left with the feeling of being in a small, dirty town. Occasional trips to the post office in the main square gave us glimpses of another Lima, one with tall buildings, large hotels and fine restaurants, but for the most part we ate in the tiny cafes near the Plaza. Our contact with the natives was limited to the poor Indians who came by the hundreds from the *barriadas* on the surrounding hillsides to see the show, and the hordes of beggar children who scrounged around the arena.

Separated from supermarkets and proper refrigeration, we had to adapt to local food conditions. The dogs were no problem; we learned quickly that the universal Latin American dish arroz con pollo, chicken with rice, made excellent meals for them. But the shortage of raw meat created problems with the cats. Each morning I

107

went to the nearby outdoor market, where the local farmers sold the biggest vegetables we had ever seen but where the day's meat offering disappeared very early in the morning. The first time I got to the chicken stall at 7:30 and found it closed, I made a private arrangement with the woman in charge. In exchange for free admission to the circus, and a couple of *soles* over the normal price, she held three chickens for me every morning until eight o'clock.

The audiences loved us. We were puzzled and delighted to see that it was our eight-minute adagio, done before the illusions and the appearance of the animals, that seemed to give them the greatest pleasure. Every day Joy had to delay the act for a few minutes by taking bows so that I could pick up all the flowers lying on the stage before the animals emerged and spooked at the unfamiliar objects in their path.

Everywhere we went Joy's platinum hair drew a crowd. Women were constantly stopping her in the street and begging her to let their children touch her hair. Each afternoon she exercised the dogs at the far end of the arena, and the street children never failed to gather there to watch. Joy took to putting on a little dog show, using the tricks that our shepherds, Sinbad and Diamond, had learned over the years, and the children screamed with delight when Sinbad sat up and begged or jumped over Diamond's back or said "Mama" when Joy put her hand under his mouth.

Our popularity with the audiences was good for us, good for the other acts, and good for Pedro's circus. It did nothing to enhance our standing with the other groups scattered around the city, and that standing hit a new low when, halfway through the Lima engagement, we won virtually every award in the competition: best music, best lighting, best choreography, best animal act, best costumes, most popular act. The acrobatic team from Bulgaria seemed to resent us far out of proportion to the circumstances, and went out of their way to let us know their feelings, including spitting at our feet every chance they got. They complained to the officials that we had contrived to rig the awards, and they muttered incessantly about our being "capitalists," as though somehow the recognition of our act had been a slap in the face of communism. The situation was not improved, either, when we were invited to the palace for tea with the president's wife. At the time we had no way of knowing that this innocent event would come back to haunt us.

On the night of August 20, we were performing before the usual crowd of about 16,000. I put the collar on Adonis and was guiding him up to the mirror ball for his sit-up when what looked like a palmetto bug the size of a mouse scurried under his nose. He leaned toward it, sniffed, and then gobbled it down. I made a mental note to tell Joy what a silly thing he had done. But almost immediately Adonis began shaking and stumbling. He fell on his side and began foaming at the mouth. Something was dreadfully wrong. I shouted to a stagehand to pull the magic cage out of sight so that Joy could come out of hiding. As the audience fell into silence, I knelt over the cat. I knew he was dying.

Adonis was dead before we got him off the stage. A beautiful and rare animal, the product of long hours of devoted training, was reduced to a lifeless thing, its face contorted with convulsions. We remember almost nothing from that first, sleepless night spent with his body, except an overpowering sense of loss and bewilderment. Joy was inconsolable, sobbing and wringing her hands in despair. The local newspapers later wrote that "the Holidays have no children. The leopard was their son." Even this was probably an understatement.

In the morning the local vet arrived. He didn't seem very knowledgeable, and he puzzled over Adonis' body for a while, remarking that in his opinion only old age, a heart attack or poison could have killed him. Finally he performed an autopsy and announced that what Adonis had eaten was not a palmetto bug but a meatball loaded with enough strychnine to kill an elephant.

As if to add to our misery that morning, the photographers from the local newspapers kept trying to get to us. We stayed out of sight in the truck with Adonis and the vet. But one cameraman managed to scale an eight-foot wall and take the most distressing pictures of Joy, her hair in curlers for the first show, weeping over Adonis' body. Every afternoon paper in the country carried that picture.

Pedro, having no sense of the fitness of things, tried to make a little extra publicity out of the whole thing by having a clown in a sad face pose with us and the cat's body. Joy went into a rage, screaming at the poor clown that his presence was totally inappropriate. Later, the man came to us and explained that Pedro had threatened to fire him if he didn't do as he was told, and Joy felt terrible that she'd given him such a hard time.

As if we weren't already in a state of shock, we now had to address the practical side of the issue. When we return from overseas with our cats, we are allowed to "reimport" them with the permits we have from the U.S. Department of the Interior. We have to be able to prove that they are the same cats we left with—their markings are like fingerprints—and if a cat dies overseas we have to be able to prove that we haven't sold or otherwise disposed of it in a manner that violates the many regulations governing possession of an endangered species. Someone at the arena now arranged for a couple of locals to skin Adonis, and then he drove Joy to the far side of the city to a taxidermist so the hide could be tanned. No sooner was the pelt in her hands than the two locals approached me for permission to take away the carcass for food. I guess if I hadn't been so insane with grief and rage I would have agreed—after all it wasn't an unreasonable request—but I shrieked a refusal at them and demanded that they burn the body immediately. The memory of the smell of that cat in the fire stays with me to this day.

We will never be convinced that it wasn't someone from the Bulgarian crew who poisoned our beautiful cat. But it was pitch dark in the arena, and no one ever came forward to point a finger. The Peruvian people went out of their way to tell us how bad they felt and how they were

110

sure no one from their country was responsible. Some even came up to us and said they would somehow get us another cat, which is patently ridiculous—Adonis was an African leopard—but we appreciated the gesture. Even in this moment of total despair, Joy carried on. Thanks to her perseverance and Demi's robotlike ability to do anything and everything under all circumstances, we didn't miss a show. Called into duty to do not only his own job but Adonis' as well, the jaguar performed beautifully. When Joy christened him her "fighter," she knew what she was talking about.

As our stay in Lima neared its end, the city suffered the sort of political convulsion that seems to regularly afflict every country south of the border. We stepped out of a restaurant one day to see shopkeepers hastily locking up their stores and pedestrians hurrying out of sight. Our backgrounds in Biddeford, Maine, gave us no experience by which to understand that a coup d'état was in progress, but our instinct told us this wasn't a happy moment, so we scurried back to our room in the Plaza.

The city held its breath for a few hours and then came back to life. President Juan Velasco Alvarado had been ousted by Gen. Francisco Morales Bermudez in what the *New York Times* referred to as an "apparently bloodless military coup." Except for the odd tank parked in an incongruous place, like the middle of a square, the city seemed to return to normal. We prepared to depart for Arequipa.

Pedro advised us that while the rest of the circus would be flying out, we would have to go by truck, because of our many heavy pieces. In this macho part of the world, there was no discussion about Joy driving. Women don't do things like that in South America, never mind that she had driven our van through all kinds of climates and terrains, over thousands and thousands of miles. So a Peruvian peasant was presented to us as a driver. At least this time the truck was large enough to carry in one trip the cat, the cages, the dogs, the trunks and all the other paraphernalia, including the four-poster bed, which gave us a rather gypsylike appearance. The one problem was that this wasn't a closed vehicle. The sides consisted of slats of wood, separated by big gaps, the back was strung with two chains, and worst of all, the top was totally open to the elements. Joy had to get down on her knees, literally, to wring a canvas out of Pedro. I kept remembering all his easy promises and the contract, and I gnashed my teeth in frustration.

With Adonis' skin carefully rolled up and placed in the back of the truck, we set off at ten at night for the long drive to Arequipa. We were still numb from the events of August 20 and were having a hard time enjoying anything or anyone around us. The driver was a taciturn soul. He stared glumly over his steering wheel, his face expressionless, his attitude one of total resignation. Despite his rather morbid presence, things began rather well. There must have been a good moon or plenty of starlight that night, because we could see our surroundings quite clearly. The drive began over a wide, paved, rather attractive road that wound up into the lower Andes. But as the altitude increased, the road narrowed, then lost its paving, and in the darkness we could see that there was barely room for a single car, let alone a truck. When we rounded curves, the front of the truck was pointed precariously into space. Most of the time large portions of the wheels on my side were hanging over the edge of a bottomless ravine. Our driver didn't help by occasionally emerging from his torpor long enough to mutter something about how dangerous the road was at this point or that. Joy and I clenched hands until our knuckles hurt.

As we climbed into the clouds, and a ghostly mist came and went around us, the temperature began to plunge, so at one of the many checkpoints along the way where our passports were examined, Joy put on all the extra clothing she could. Tights went over the stockings, leg warmers went over the tights, slacks went over the leg warmers, and finally, in desperation, she put on the mink coat. A good part of the cold we were enduring was undoubtedly the fear that at any minute all of us could be plunged into nothingness. I tried not to think about the fact that in order to get back to Lima we were going to have to make this trip all over again in two weeks. As the night grew later, our driver seemed determined to take a nap, apparently indifferent to the fact that his hands on the steering wheel were the only things between us and our Maker. His chin kept trying to make contact with his chest. It was obvious he couldn't keep his eyes open, and since he refused to make conversation, we were at a loss to keep him alert. Finally Joy discovered that he liked candy, and she plied him from time to time with strawberry-flavored lumps in the hope that the exercise of chewing would discourage him from dropping into a deep slumber. Every time I saw his eyes closing I wanted to reach across Joy and sock him, but on this narrow, frightening road in the middle of nowhere, it didn't seem the prudent thing to do. I held on to Joy's hand and imagined the grievous bodily damage I was going to perpetrate on Pedro if I survived this trip. It was inconceivable to me that he would have exposed us and our valuable cargo to such a treacherous journey.

At the lower elevations we had noticed several crosses planted in the ground along the outer edge of the road, apparently marking the sites of tragic accidents. Now, as we climbed higher, the crosses seemed in the darkness to be more roughly made, like two chunks of wood held together with rope. Every now and then we saw one that had a strange, round object atop it, but in the swirling mist we couldn't tell what we were looking at. Sometimes there would be one such cross, sometimes a whole group. Finally the driver opened his eyes and mouth long enough to explain that these were the decapitated heads of people who had died in motor accidents on this road. If their bodies were recoverable, and if their relatives could afford to pay for the retrieving, their heads were removed and placed on crude crosses along the edge of the road as a warning to others not to be reckless. This information, relayed in a matter-of-fact style, added a case of the horrors to our numbness, bringing a nightmarish quality to a journey that was already unbearable.

Some of the heads were merely skulls; others appeared to be recent additions. Through the mist I even saw a large bird perched on one. It was certainly a peculiar custom in a Catholic country, but in these remote areas the ancient Indian superstitions still took precedence over the church.

Suddenly we rounded a curve and saw a mass of flickering lights up ahead. "We must stop here," the driver said, pulling up before a tiny chapel. "If we don't light a candle, we won't make it over the top." We weren't about to argue with him. Inside, the candles were literally everywhere, so thick on the floor we had to step carefully between them to reach the supply near the altar. All along the walls were more heads, some of them preserved under glass, others just lying there, rotting. Nausea swept over us, but I grabbed at least four candles and quickly lit them.

As we fled back to the truck, I whispered to Joy, "Remember this—because nobody is ever going to believe it."

The beginnings of daylight gave us some hope that we might yet survive but also provided us with the grisly sight of a schoolbus lying at the bottom of a very deep ravine. It looked as though someone had taken it by either end and twisted. The bodies of the children lay everywhere, some thrown away from the bus, others hanging half-in, half-out of the windows. We stared in shock and disbelief, our first thought for the unlucky ones who hadn't died immediately, because it was obvious that this was where the bus and its occupants were going to stay. Only a helicopter could have reached it and in these parts there was no such thing. "You see, you see," pointed the driver, triumphantly. "They didn't light a candle."

We drove on in silence, watching the day slowly bring form and substance to our surroundings, and then suddenly the sun sprang over a distant hill and we could see the Pacific Ocean. It was a glorious sight and we breathed a sigh of relief that must have been heard in Paraguay. The events of the previous night quickly dimmed; surely we had dreamed it all.

Despite a bellyful of candy, our driver was hungry, and as we came to the desertlike lowlands, he pulled the truck up to a tiny, unappetizing restaurant. Food was the last thing on our minds—our stomachs were still tied in knots from the sights we had seen. But we had to go to the bathroom something awful. We were in a very sparsely populated area, with slightly hilly dunes here and there and almost no vegetation. There was no one around, so we wandered a respectable distance from the restaurant and Joy went through the process of peeling down the layers of tights and stockings. She hoisted her mink up behind her and squatted down while I stood watch. Suddenly we heard a scrabbling noise and out of nowhere came a pack of wild dogs, snarling and growling and obviously underfed. I grabbed Joy as she sat, both of us oblivious of hygiene, ran like a madman, threw her over the back of the truck and hauled myself in as the dogs began to close the distance between us. Behind us our own dogs were making defensive noises on our behalf and it was all we could do to restrain them. The wild dogs grew closer, so that we could see how thin and mangy they were. They seemed certain to jump into the truck with us, when an old man stepped out of the restaurant and fired three shots in the air. The dogs melted away. As we lay there shaking with fear and rage, we wondered why nobody had had the decency to warn us.

Reeking of urine, we reached Arequipa after fourteen wretched hours. This city was a much nicer place than Lima, at least from our point of view. It was cleaner and less dusty, and had plenty of daily sunshine. The air sparkled at 7,500 feet above sea level, and the volcano *El Misti* in the distance was an enchanting sight. The circus was set up in a concrete building that served as a sort of sports center for the local schools. Had it not been for the daily reminder that our beloved Adonis had been reduced to a tanned pelt, we probably would have enjoyed Arequipa immensely. News of our loss had reached this part of the country as well, and we were constantly assured that the Peruvian people were not responsible.

115

Demetrius was sick almost every day in Arequipa. There was no chicken and no beef, only alpaca meat, which must have been too strong for his system. This was ironic: a Brazilian jaguar who was unable to stomach the cuisine in a South American country. Trouper that he is, he performed up to snuff for each show, and had the decency to be sick backstage.

After the circus' two-week engagement in Arequipa was up, I informed Pedro that under no circumstances were we to be driven back to Lima over the same route we had come on. As a result of my insistence, the drive back wasn't nearly as bad as we expected. The road was still very hilly but nowhere near as treacherous as before, and this trip was made largely in daylight. To this day, when we look at maps of Peru, we are baffled as to why our driver didn't use the good old, reliable Panamerican Highway, which runs smoothly along the coast south toward Arequipa. The only explanation that makes sense, assuming the lack of malice, is that he thought he was doing us a favor. With the military junta only a few days in power, it is quite likely that the main roads were clogged with troop movements.

We had the same driver on the return trip but we were ready for him, and Joy kept the strawberry chewies coming. This time he didn't get groggy until we were on the main road to Lima.

As soon as we could we made it very clear to Pedro that we were ready to go *home*. He acquiesced and told us he needed a day or two to make our flight arrangements. Since there was no way we could stay in a hotel and still be close to our animals, Pedro managed to find a place for us in the spare room of a mechanic's shop near the center of the city. The mechanic and his family were wonderful to us, and we could keep a constant eye on the truck and our property. It wasn't a bad arrangement, with use of the bed and the hot-water device, and it was only to be for a day or two while Pedro arranged for our return passage.

As we were settling into our new quarters, Pedro's sister stopped by to tell us that we could expect a visit from

116

the military, because we had been to the palace to have tea with the wife of the man they had recently deposed. We interpreted this as merely an expression of the family's dismal personalities, but she knew what she was talking about. The next day, two humorless men in uniform were at our door, searching our luggage and making threatening noises. We explained that we were only hanging about in anticipation of our tickets home, which seemed to please them, because one of them made some crack about getting us out of the country before we could "do any more damage." He also referred to us as "enemies of the state."

While searching our luggage, our two visitors came across a pile of *soles* representing the $8,000 American we had been paid by Pedro. A lot of hand-waving went on to indicate that we obviously intended to flee the country without paying our taxes. So we were escorted to an official building of some sort, where a conversation with the bureaucrat in charge left no doubt that the new government was after most, if not all, of our money.

Finding ourselves temporarily free of our escorts, we went to the American embassy, guided by that common but erroneous belief that our country's representatives would be able to wave a magic wand and clear the path of all obstacles. Their hands were tied; they could not interfere in any way. And sure enough, when we went back to pay the taxes, it was a simple exchange: We gave them all our money and they gave us back the passports they had confiscated at the garage.

At last we were told that we could go to the airport for the weighing process that would allow Pedro to calculate our air fares and purchase the tickets. Under the impression that our departure was only hours away, we loaded everything into a truck and, under military escort, drove out to the Lima airport. After nine pieces of luggage were weighed, we were shown to an outbuilding and the dogs, the cat, and our other pieces were put into a small room. It seemed like a logical place to store everything until the cargo plane was ready, but as we stepped out of the room one of the soldiers pointed to me and said, "Not you. We don't know what you'll get up to back in Lima, so you're staying here."

I protested that it was unreasonable to ask my wife to wander alone around Lima, but the soldiers were adamant. Since one of them was brandishing a semiautomatic weapon, I gave in. I was told that Joy could come in the morning with food for me and the animals, which raised a lot of unasked questions about exactly how long they planned to keep me under lock and key.

Years later I would tell people about the five or six days I spent under arrest in Peru, but then one day I hauled out a shopping bag full of receipts and old airline-ticket stubs and found to my amazement that I was there only three days. My concept of time, never good under the best of circumstances, had been further befuddled by my inability to distinguish night from day. The room had only one little window, in the door, looking out into a dimly lit hallway. Moreover, there was no routine by which I could judge time. I tried to sleep, but I was so worried about Joy, and about the guards suddenly deciding that I or my animals were some sort of threat, that I slept for only a few minutes at a time. I was given a bucket of water for whatever purposes I saw fit. There was no toilet in the room and the guard had made it quite clear that I would regret using the floor. So when the bucket arrived each day I got the animals to drink, took a little myself, and then held out until as late in the day as possible before using it for a potty. I doubted very much that the bucket was being cleaned before being refilled, but I chose not to ask.

I was also told that if the guard ever opened the door and saw Demi strolling about the room, he would shoot on sight. I decided it was better for Demi to forgo exercise than to wind up like the skin of Adonis that was rolled up on top of one of the cages. (My guardians had made an attempt to confiscate the skin, using as an excuse the words of a misguided reporter who had written in the Lima paper that we intended to donate it to the Museum

118

of Natural History. They had not reckoned with Joy. Despite their weapons, she had stepped forward and hissed at them between clenched teeth, "Over my dead body." They didn't mention the skin again.)

The intriguing feature of my otherwise barren chamber was a pile of gold bars set against one wall. I often had the feeling that the guards at the door were more intent on protecting that valuable hoard than on preventing my escape. I was very pleased with Sinbad one day when he strolled over and lifted a leg against the glittering heap—it was such a satisfying gesture.

Each morning Joy arrived with food for all of us prisoners. The guard at the door, for whom I adopted a most unchristian loathing, carefully selected the choice piece from my portion, then passed Joy through. While I ate, she took the two dogs out on the airstrip for exercise, an activity which, despite our bizarre situation, gave her a lift and an inexplicable feeling of importance.

Finally one afternoon Joy was told by Pedro that she should get out to the airport because there was "good news." The military was going to let me fly out the next day. That was the last time either of us saw the unlovable Pedro. But now we had another problem. Somehow, when the soldiers searched our property, they overlooked about $1200 in *soles* that Joy had tucked away in her purse. We had been sternly warned about the illegality of taking Peruvian money out of the country, but we were also forbidden to change the *soles* into dollars. Unless we did something drastic, we were going to arrive home without a cent between us. When Joy paid her pre-departure visit that afternoon, I told her she was going to have to find a way to convert the *soles* into gold suitable for smuggling out of the country. We both realized how dangerous this was, but by now we were fed up with Peru and were feeling reckless.

The next morning Joy went into downtown Lima and wandered up and down looking in the windows of jewelry shops. Finally, on impulse, she strolled into one of them and told the manager she wanted to buy gold. He offered

119

her bracelets and earrings and the like, until she got up the nerve to tell him what she had in mind. He looked at her. "You're Señora Holiday, aren't you?" That was the first time being recognized really paid off. The jeweler expressed his sympathy for the loss of Adonis and his desire to help right the wrong. "What you're asking is extremely illegal," he said, "but if you leave the money with me and come back after siesta, I'll see what I can do."

It wasn't an easy decision, but Joy realized that the *soles* were probably worthless anyway. So she left the money, wondering if the manager would go straight to the telephone and turn her in. In the middle of the afternoon, she stood in the shadows across the street, making sure the military weren't lurking about. Seeing nothing to cause suspicion, she took a deep breath and, on wobbling legs, entered the store, where to her horror she saw not a single person who had been there that morning. She was sure she'd been had, and was about to leave when she heard her name and turned around to see the manager signaling her from his office. He took her inside, closed the door, and handed her a gold rectangle about the size of a candy bar. "I don't care how you get it out of the country," he said, "but hide it somewhere very, very safe." Deeply grateful, Joy thanked him and, tucking the bar into her bra, went back to her room and carefully sewed it into the crotch of her underpants.

Later that evening we were presented with airline tickets, but not before the military gave us one more show. I was taken out of the room with my wrists handcuffed behind me, then two guards went back into the room and closed the door behind them. Joy and I and another guard stood in the hallway for what seemed like an hour. Our new watchdog was a lot more humane than I was used to, even to the point of offering me a cigarette, and he explained with silent gestures that his compatriots were checking each and every bar to make sure I hadn't scraped off some of the gold and hidden it in my clothing. There was no way to make any of them understand that I was a great deal more interested in getting

120

my pets, my wife and myself out of their damned country, alive and well, than in collecting a few bits of gold dust. How they would have shrieked if they'd known about the bar in Joy's undies.

As the hour for my departure approached, I was terrified at the idea of leaving Joy behind, especially with that incriminating gold bar. I hadn't liked flying into Peru on separate carriers, and now had no faith whatsoever that both of us would get out of there. Once my plane left the ground Joy would be totally unprotected. What's more, when we had paid our taxes, we had been given only one exit card, and our pleadings for another fell on deaf ears. Joy took what she considered the sensible approach ("you and the animals are more important than me") and pressed the card on me. She realized that she would probably have a major battle on her hands at the airport, and I wondered if I would ever see her again. At midnight, when my plane took off, my heart was absolutely bursting with fear, and I spent the entire flight in a state of inconsolable misery.

Joy did indeed have a hard time at the gate, and had to explain over and over that her husband had just left on a cargo flight with our only exit card. After endless telephone calls, the officials decided she was telling the truth and saw fit to pass her through to the waiting area.

She took a seat next to an American man and was feeling a little less tense when she spotted an airline attendant moving among the other passengers with an odd-looking device. She asked the American what was going on. "Oh," he replied, "that's a metal detector. Lan Chile is very careful about skyjackers."

A cold sweat trickled down Joy's back as the attendant checked the American and then moved on to her. The metal detector was passed up and down her left arm, down and up her left leg, and was being passed to her right leg when it went off with a scream that to Joy sounded like the end of the world. She was about to leap to her feet and confess all, when the examiner reached into her travel bag and pulled out an alarm clock, nod-

121

ding with satisfaction at having found the offending metal. With legs like jelly, Joy boarded the plane.

Flying back to Miami on our separate aircraft, we both had one concern: Had the other actually taken off? I had inquired the moment my plane set down, and had been informed that Joy was airborne, or at least the plane she was supposed to be on had left the ground. She in turn asked the stewardess for information, and was grateful to the crew for radioing ahead and learning that my plane was approaching Miami.

I was amazed when I landed to see not only the usual customs officials board the plane but also two men who turned out to be from the FBI. They somehow knew all about the poisoning of Adonis, and while they didn't say they knew about my three days in solitary, they seemed to know that I had had a rough time. Perhaps they got a clue when I knelt down on the tarmac and kissed the American ground. In any event, they were wonderful to me. They helped me get the animals and equipment off the plane, asked me where I wanted to go, got me some fried chicken, drove me down the street to rent a truck for the ride to St. Petersburg, and then asked me what I wanted to do.

"See that tree over there?" I pointed. "I want to sit there in the shade with my pets, thank God I'm back in my own country, relax and wait for my wife."

Joy had one more hurdle. When she came through customs and presented her passport, the official looked at it and mumbled, "Something is very irregular here." The sight of a man in uniform about to give her another hard time almost broke her. Holding her breath, she asked what the problem was. "Madam," he said, "according to this passport you've been gone three months, and yet all your luggage consists of is this," waving at her purse and her cosmetic case. "Now, don't try to tell me you spent three months in Peru with only two little pieces."

Joy began to explain about her husband, the cargo plane, the cats, when the official interrupted. "Oh!" he exclaimed, "you're the one." And she was hustled through. Later, when we compared notes of the return trip, it seemed that everyone at the Miami airport knew about us.

Joy put her two pieces of luggage under her arm and walked out of the airport, determined not to lose her composure so close to home. When she saw me just across the road, she disintegrated, tears of relief rolling down her face at the sight of us, safe and healthy under a tree that wasn't blackened with dust.

The ride back to St. Petersburg was strained. Between bits of conversation designed to find out how the other had fared, we cried, talked some more, cried some more. Our house looked like heaven on earth. We locked the doors, disconnected the telephone, and hid.

7

No sooner had we bounced back from the nightmare of Peru, bloody, broke, but unbeaten, than we were booked for another international appearance, this time as part of a revue at the El San Juan Hotel, in Puerto Rico. It should have been a perfectly straightforward trip, but Heaven forbid we should ever just pack up, go, perform, and come back without having a little sidetrip through the twilight zone!

Our passage on the freighter *Puerto Rico*, out of Jacksonville, was prepaid, and when we saw the bill of lading we were grateful it was someone else's problem. The minimum number of animals for transport was ten; with the cats and dogs we had only four, leaving at the bottom of the ticket a whopping charge for what was whimsically called a "six animal deficit."

The freighter seemed immense to us—I was sure the prow would dock in San Juan before the stern left Jacksonville. Its decks and holds were crammed from one end to the other with "reefers," refrigerated semis to haul overland whatever Puerto Rico must import, which is just about everything. A high, wide superstructure at the stern housed the crew, the officers, and the dining quarters, with an elevator connecting the various levels to the deck and holds. It was to our advantage that passengers were a rarity on this ship, because the only accommodations deemed suitable for us were the owner's rather lavish quarters, high in the superstructure. Murphy (or one of his Latin cousins) being in charge, our van, trailer and animals ended up as far from us as possible—we were high up in the stern, they were in the first hold in the prow, with all those semis in between. But they were protected from the elements, and all our equipment was tightly lashed down, so we couldn't really complain.

This was a working trip, and we had no illusions about a romantic sea voyage, moonlight on the water, and all that soggy stuff. Still, our first sight of the deck was a bit of a shock. Unlike the big cruise ships, with their concern for passenger safety, the freighter had only a double row of chains strung between posts to discourage the crew from falling overboard. During rough weather that deck must have been terrifying. But the first day out the sea was calm; the animals settled in nicely, we were enjoying the salt air. The only odd thing was the absence of people. There had to be a fairly sizable crew on that ship but we rarely saw anyone. Somewhere below decks all sorts of activity was probably going on, but we saw no sign of it and often felt as though we were on a phantom ship.

Not everyone was invisible. There was one young crewman who took a fancy to Sinbad and spent his every free minute hanging around the van. This was rather a shame because no one ever accused Sinbad of being man's best friend, and he defied the sailor's efforts to win his affection. The boy brought him all sorts of treats, which Sinbad spurned unless we were standing right there with nods of approval. We didn't go out of our way to encourage the friendship because the last thing we needed was a tail-wagging, hand-licking guard dog.

On the first night things began to fall apart. In our cabin after dinner, Joy had her nose in a book and I was making minor repairs to the costumes, when our ears picked up sounds so eerie they made our hair literally stand on end. "Oooooo," and then "Ahhhhhh," and then "Ohhhhhh," softly sometimes, as though from a great distance, and louder at others, as though right outside our portholes. Certain that these sounds had human origin, I kept opening the door and peering up and down the passageway, but there was no one around. Joy kept saying, "Ron, what is that?" I hadn't the faintest idea.

About nine o'clock we took a welcome break from this weirdness and went down into the hold to feed the dogs and cats. It was not pleasant stepping out of the elevator. The cavernous hold was a world of shadows, lit only by a few dim bulbs and our flashlight. The reefers, black hulks hunkering in the darkness, made us feel very small and vulnerable. The dogs weren't happy, either. Instead of lolling about dreaming dog-dreams, they were lying glumly wide awake, noses on paws, eyes rolling restlessly up and down and side to side. They looked worried. Demi seemed to be all right; if he was acting strangely, it was only because we were projecting our own disquiet onto him. Only baby Venus was sound asleep.

Joy resorted to a few quick shots of rum to induce sleep, something she never does, but we spent a fitful night trying to drown out the wailings and moanings. At breakfast we asked one of the officers about the sounds but he assured us it was only the wind in the rigging. We didn't bother to mention that we had been out on deck during the evening and the sea was so flat the ship seemed to be floating above it.

And now, in broad daylight, the dogs were howling, their noses pointed upward, baying like beagles. We tried to exercise them, but even after we'd dragged them out they refused to move. They stood firmly at our feet, as though glued to the deck, shivering and quaking, and in despair we put them back in their cages.

We were, of course, in the Bermuda Triangle. No one will ever be able to convince us that the hullaballoo about this geographical phenomenon is nonsense.

On the second night, events took a bizarre turn. We were very reluctant to take our late evening ride down to the animals. Although the wailings and howlings seemed to have ceased, we kept imagining we heard them, straining our ears against the normal engine noises so that it became hard to tell which sounds were real and which were inside our own heads. As frightening as our cabin was, we hesitated to leave its relative safety for the intimidating world of the semis. But the animals had to be fed. Holding tightly to each other, we rode down in the elevator and tiptoed through the hold, waving the flashlight around wildly at the monster shadows we were creating. At the van, things were as the night before, the cats quiet and subdued, the dogs restless and watchful. We passed out the food, gave a few reassuring pats on their furry heads, and then picked our way back to the elevator.

I pushed the button for our cabin level, some five stories up, and the elevator began to rise. It went a couple of feet, made a loud, whirring noise, and, after a bounce or two, came to a complete halt. We looked at each other in dismay. Our nerves were bad enough; we didn't need to spend the night stuck in an elevator. I gave the doors a push and they parted. Greatly relieved, I helped Joy down the two-foot jump to the deck and was about to follow her when I felt something splash on my head. I looked up, aimed the flashlight, and saw something dripping from the little hatchway in the top of the cab. "Joy?" I said, turning toward her with the flashlight in my hand.

"Ron!" she screamed. "You've got blood all over your face!"

What we did then is rather embarrassing and thoroughly cowardly, but understandable in light of our experience in Peru. We ran up the five flights to our cabin, bolted the door, cleaned me up, and went to bed. We had no idea what had happened in that elevator and we didn't want to know. We downed as much rum as we could lay our hands on, but it didn't help. All night we lay awake in our bunks, trying not to listen for the night voices and wondering what had been in the elevator shaft. We were so unnerved I don't think we would have been surprised to see a pair of disembodied hands rapping on the porthole.

We stayed in our cabin in the morning, unwilling to face the day. A steward finally tapped on the door and came in with a tray of coffee. "Did you hear about the accident last night?" he asked, eagerly. We feigned ignorance. "Remember that little guy who was always hanging around your dog? He got his head crushed in the elevator shaft." Nausea swept over us, but the steward wasn't finished. "We got his body in the refrigerator. You want to see it? You can identify him for the police when we dock." We turned down this offer.

It seems our little friend had hidden drugs of some sort between the decks and had been in the process of retrieving them when we pushed the button. We'll never know why he didn't have enough sense to shut down the elevator before climbing into the shaft. In any event, we decided to lay low. With our first performance only hours away, we couldn't afford to get involved in a lengthy investigation. To this day we feel uneasy that we didn't step forward, but we are somewhat consoled by the knowledge that our admission would have changed nothing.

* * *

We felt a lot better when we had left the ship behind and settled into the El San Juan Hotel. Management had provided us with our own lanai, an efficiency apartment with patio right on the beach. This arrangement kept us a considerable distance from the animals, who were housed in the van at the rear of the hotel, but they were safe behind a concrete wall, and the hotel guards, except on one memorable and unfortunate occasion, proved to be extremely vigilant about their welfare. Rumor had it that a favorite local pastime was burglarizing the lanais, so we chose to take the dogs off guarding the cats and put them in charge of watching the apartment. Our hearts sank when we saw the Tropicoro Room, where we were to perform. The ceiling was far too low. Had we tried to do the adagio lifts in that room, Joy would have ended up hanging from the lighting fixtures. The hotel manager set about at once to make alterations. With this problem worrying us, the last thing we needed was the previous act to show up at our elbow—an elderly German man with a chimp act who was driving the producer crazy by telling anti-Semitic jokes on stage. Word had come down from the top: "Come up with something better." We were the something better, and the old man, eager to spoil our fun, spent a lot of time hanging about, painting a dismal picture of the El San Juan and the working conditions.

He was sitting in the supper club one day when we arrived to walk Demi around for a bit of acclimating. The waiters were busily preparing the tables for the night's audience, which was to be the last for the old man. Demi reached the stage and immediatly set about marking off his territory, spraying urine for twenty feet in all directions. The waiters scurried for cover as the old man let out a hoot of joy and squealed, "Dot's gonna hoppen efry night! You see, you gonna get sued!"

The producer took Demi's natural behavior in stride and even joked with the waiters, saying, "If you have any enemies in the audience tomorrow, seat them down front."

The old man's hope for our failure came to naught. We went to Puerto Rico with a 19-week contract and did so well that our option was picked up over and over and we ended up spending nearly a year there. The show, *Viva Carnaval*, was a hit, and the working conditions were really quite good.

Not everything went like clockwork. There was one bit of nonsense that will stay in our minds forever as a classic example of what can go wrong when communication breaks down. During a performance one night we spotted a familiar face in the audience, a neighbor named Mr. McDowell. After our act, as we waited to appear for a bow with little Venus, we made a note to seek him out and give him a nice welcome. This was the main thing on our minds when we came out for the finale. As we bowed to the audience, Joy heard one of the more flighty showgirls behind us scream, "Oh my God, he's loose!" I didn't hear her, and at that very second, as the curtain came down for the last time, I said to Joy, "You stay here, I'll go look for him." Joy, assuming I had heard the showgirl's scream, flew into a panic. Instead of understanding me to mean I was going in search of Mr. McDowell, she took my words as confirmation that Demi had escaped. Simultaneously, pandemonium erupted behind us as the showgirl began screeching in fear while trying to climb up on the piano, the huge feathers on her hips rapping a tattoo on the helpless piano player's face, while another dancer, catching on to the problem, began to scramble up on the drums. Joy saw all this in a flash as she raced backstage in search of Demi—and stopped dead in her tracks when she found him lying on his back in his cage, sound asleep, paws draped in the air.

The showgirl, not the brightest of creatures, had peered into the cage on her way out for the finale, and had actually managed not to see the big cat. Joy read her the riot act for causing such a scene over nothing. Now we look back and laugh when we picture that piano player trying to brush the feathers out of his face. And when we remember that the man in the audience wasn't Mr. McDowell at all but a comedian we had worked with many years before.

* * *

Demi got sick in Puerto Rico. Joy was in the middle of cuing him for his leap through a hoop when he suddenly bent down and snuggled his head on her chest. Instantly she knew something was wrong, but she talked him through it, calling him her "Sugar Bear" and coaxing him into completing the performance. Back in his cage, he kept making yawning movements with his mouth and

Joy thought perhaps there was something stuck in his throat. He allowed her to pry his mouth open and poke around up to her elbow, but she found nothing. She was to remember how trusting and cooperative he was that day when, a few weeks later, her relationship with the jaguar took on quite a different complexion.

We were a long way from our vet in St. Petersburg, and the prospect of trusting a rare and beloved animal to a stranger was frightening. But after lengthy telephone inquiries we located a vet who had experience with big cats. More the pity for him, because he took one look at Demi and knew exactly what he was dealing with. He grew very quiet. With pursed lips and furrowed brow he stared glumly at the cat until Joy, growing impatient, asked him, "What would you like to do?"

The vet tugged uneasily at his collar. "Ah, um, I'd like to look down his throat."

"No problem." Joy pried Demi's mouth open, pulled his tongue out a bit, and waved on the vet.

With a few cautious steps the doctor came as close as he dared, craned his neck, said "Thank you," and withdrew. "He has the flu," he announced. No doubt it was the same bug that had been laying low a lot of two-legged residents at the hotel. Antibiotics concealed in meatballs, which Demi wolfed down with a hearty appetite, soon had him on his feet again.

* * *

As we entered the last sixteen weeks of our engagement, we were following a magic act that featured birds bursting out of balloons. When that act left the stage, the floor was littered with bits of balloon fragments, and Joy tried very hard to convince the stage manager that these were a hazard to us. But he was adamant that there wasn't enough time to sweep the stage during the blackout between acts, and we were forced to work around the litter. And the inevitable happened. One night, as Joy slid into a split from her double-tuck somersault, her foot stopped short on a bit of balloon, but her leg kept going.

131

At first we thought the damage would be minimal and short-term. The next morning the knee was a little tender but not unworkable, and we got through the performances without any problems. Joy had been working for days with a bad arm, anyway. Demi, who had not yet reached his full dimensions, was outgrowing his compartment in the magic cage, and one night the trapdoor broke as he squeezed through. Joy was pinned against a metal plate, unable to get free because Demi was standing on the trapdoor. The arm was badly bruised but not broken, a factor the doctor attributed to the strong muscles Joy has from doing handstands and lifts.

By the second day it was obvious that Joy wasn't going to escape with a bruised knee. It was so swollen and painful that she couldn't stand even the weight of a sheet on it. The next sixteen weeks saw a constant round of visits to doctors, who drew off liquid and made things better for a few days, and then the problem would recur. The doctors kept saying, "If you can stand the pain, go ahead and work on it," and Joy kept saying, "Listen, you don't know what you're saying." When it comes to a choice between performing and nursing wounds, Joy doesn't think twice. But she was concerned about doing permanent damage to herself. She didn't miss a single performance because of the knee, although the pain during the disappearing illusion was so excruciating that her flight from the stage to throw up became a regular, nightly thing.

Almost immediately after the accident the stage manager had a sudden change of heart and miraculously found a few seconds in which to sweep the stage during the blackout. All the same, we weren't surprised when, on the day of our last performance, a couple of lawyers showed up at our lanai. We were about to explain that lawsuits were not our way of dealing with such problems when they informed us that they were representing the hotel in Miami and the producer there, both of whom were being sued by the juggler and his wife. The four of us spent the afternoon in the hotel's coffee shop, where I did my best to set the record straight about the woman's imaginary injuries. It was Joy who realized how late it was getting and said we had to feed our animals. The lawyers, eager to watch, accompanied us down to the van in the delivery courtyard.

We reached the cages just in time to see two young men racing away from the scene. Without the dogs to warn them off, they had got close enough to stick an unbent wire coathanger into the jaguar's cage. The weapon had torn the flesh on Demi's forehead, narrowly missing his eye. He was bleeding profusely and carrying on like a wounded bear.

I took off after the two of them, murder in my heart. With the lawyers standing by, Joy climbed into the van, and made one of the worst mistakes of her career. All the people who had told her how much Demi loved her, how he would never hurt her, had eroded her judgment, giving her a sort of silver-bullet complex about that cat. This was to be the first, and last, time she forgot that there's no such thing as a "tame" animal. Seeing him in such pain, she thought she could comfort him, so she stepped into the van and opened the cage door. Demi was not looking for solace. He was hurt, and he was going to hurt in return. He came flying out at her and began to bite wherever he could get purchase. Joy struggled to fend him off. Pinned to the floor, she managed to land a couple of blows with a hammer, which held the cat back but only temporarily. Once she nearly had him maneuvered back into his cage, but at the last minute he outsmarted her and attacked again. Close to fainting from fear and physical trauma, she managed to hang on only because she knew the door of the van was open and if she passed out, the cat would be on the loose.

Just as Joy began to suspect that she was really going to die, the jaguar inexplicably stopped and backed into his cage. With her last ounce of strength, Joy shut the door.

Unsuccessful in my pursuit, I returned in time to see Joy stagger out of the van, covered with blood and on the verge of unconsciousness. I scooped her up in my arms and raced to the lanai. Recalling the advice of Pat Anthony, a famous trainer of big cats whom we had met only weeks before, I filled my mouth with hydrogen pyroxide and blew it into the deep punctures in Joy's arm—many of the wounds had gone all the way through—and then rushed her to the hospital. Angry, confused and traumatized, she gave the doctor a very hard time, howling in pain as he cleaned her up and rejecting all offers of medication because she had a "performance to do." The doctor must have thought her demented.

Despite my misgivings, we did prepare for the performance that evening. Joy, now recuperating from one bruised arm, one bloody and bandaged arm, and one lame knee, resembled a war victim. We made some minor modifications to the act to allow for her condition—she passed up the false eyelashes, which required the use of two good hands, and we cut out bits of the adagio where she would be unable to support herself. And then we went to get Demi, the one factor we hadn't considered in our efforts to keep the show going. Unaccustomed to abuse in any form, he had reverted to his natural state, a wild thing snarling and slashing at us as though we were total strangers. We couldn't even get him out of the cage.

In the end we had to miss closing night. We sat in the audience, applauding the other acts, and Joy cried until the last curtain rang down.

A question we asked ourselves for many months after this near fatal accident was, why did Demi back off at the last minute? Recent research with cats in their natural environment may have provided one answer. It seems that exotic cats rarely, if ever, deliberately kill members of their own species. They fight only until they've made their point, and then walk away. It is reasonable to argue that Demi was behaving according to this instinct. Perceiving us as kin of some sort, or at least as the creatures he grew up with, he mauled Joy to his satisfaction and, having vented his anger, withdrew. Perhaps when people tell us that the jaguar's genuine affection for Joy overcame his momentary rage and fear, they are saying the same thing.

8

Slowly the wounds from Puerto Rico healed, and life returned to a normal routine of exercise for us and the pets. We had a couple of months of r&r before an appearance at the Chateau Champlain in Montreal, which had been delayed so that Joy could recover from her assorted injuries. Just as I had been forced to overcome my fear of Adonis after the attack in Texas, so Joy now had to face Demi. It is hard not to have an altered perception of an animal after it has taken a piece or two out of you. In the back of your mind is the nagging possibility that the cat might want to make a habit out of this sort of thing. Joy went into a stalling mode after we got home, putting off the routine of exercise and rehearsal day after day until finally I put my foot down and said, "Now! Today!" Demi, of course, performed beautifully—the problem was in Joy's head, not his. When I complimented her on how controlled she was while putting him through his paces, she confessed that it had all been an act: "My insides were like Jell-O."

The timing of our engagement in Montreal could not have been better, allowing the infant Hercules a period at home with us to get acquainted as well as exposure to our business while he was still young enough to be molded.

With our van full of felines and our trailer full of paraphernalia, we were met at the Canadian border by one of those frequently encountered types, the ordinary guy whose title and uniform have gone to his head—in this case a customs official who was determined to prove how obnoxious he could be. Without any of the common courtesies, he came striding up to our rig and shouted, "Open it!"

Joy, thinking he meant the trailer, headed off in that direction, but the inspector was moving toward the van. "Joy," I called to her, "he wants the van, not the trailer."

Joy started back toward me, calling to the man, "Watch out! I've got my cats in there," but the Authority was in a hurry. Before I could stop him, he shoved past me and opened the back door of the van, leading to the rear compartment.

In the forward compartment were Venus and Demi, in their cages. Behind them was a mesh screen that closed off the back of the van and made a nice home for the baby Hercules, who was about the size of a large dog. He spent his time there rough-housing with a small pile of blankets, as active and rambunctious as any kitten. At the Canadian border, his main concern was relieving himself. He seemed to have been born with an aversion to urinating in his cage and would hold back until he could get to newspaper or, much more preferable, grass.

Under proper circumstances the door of the van would not be opened until I had entered from the front and collared Herk. The customs man gave us no time for this routine. Hercules, rollicking among his blankets, saw the door open and had only one thought: grass. He literally flew over the inspector's shoulder and out onto the green of the highway verge, scattering blankets every which way. I dashed after him, the collar in my hand, but there was no need to panic. Feeling the grass under his paws, he promptly squatted down with that far-away, blissful look that all cats get when they go about their business.

When I got him back to the van, I found Joy standing over the prone body of the customs man. "Ron, I think there's something wrong with him."

The official was lying between the van and the trailer, making odd, strangling noises. We quickly summoned another inspector from the nearby customs building, who took one look and gasped, "My God! He's having a heart attack!"

We stood around with nothing to do but watch as an ambulance sped off with the hapless man. When the wail of the siren had died away, we dared to ask what we should do. To our astonishment, we were told to be on our way.

That night my wife seemed longer at her prayers than usual. When she finally got off her knees, I asked, "What was all that about?"

"Oh," she replied, with a straight face, "I was just praying that son of a bitch had a small heart attack, not a big one."

We held our breath for a few days, fully expecting to be summoned to some sort of inquiry, but there were no repercussions. Maybe the customs authorities realized how foolish the man had been. Even if he had misunderstood when Joy used the word "cats," whether we were carrying tigers or tabbies, he had no business summarily flinging open the door of a private vehicle. It's quite likely he never knew what had come hurtling at him.

* * *

The Chateau Champlain is the *chic de la chic* in Montreal, a really prize place to perform, even if everything there is done to wretched excess—the food, the decor, the waiters—everything and everyone was just too, too. We got the engagement because the manager had seen us perform in San Juan. The only change we made between the two cities was Hercules who, as a babe in arms for a farewell bow, couldn't exactly be called an addition to the act. Nevertheless, we bombed. Whether it was our score, which was massacred nightly by a union-choked four-piece "orchestra" of old men who couldn't even read music, or the bored, blasé jet-set crowd determined to keep eating and ignore the stage no matter what, we were anything but a hit. We had arrived in Montreal as the stars, to close the show, but after a couple of weeks of deadly performances, we were moved to the opening slot. This was so debasing that we simply put the whole affair out of our minds and concentrated on hanging on through the three months' contract and then getting the hell out of there.

Demi picked this most humiliating of times to enter an ugly stage. His male hormones were becoming active and he was frustrated. The sight of Joy, or the sound of her voice, would send him into paroxysms of feline mastur-bation, but even that didn't help, and he became very dif-ficult. Joy was reluctant to use him more than twice a day, and when the first Saturday came around, with its three performances, she substituted Venus. This was not a perfect solution. Demi, when he is at peak form, is to-tally indifferent to his environment and undisturbed by anything around him. Venus is inclined to be more highly strung. In Montreal, the group that followed us was a dog act, and Joy spent a lot of time that Saturday morning carefully explaining to the stage manager that those animals had to remain out of Venus' line of vision until the little leopard was off the stage.

Still, as Joy put Venus through her paces, she could see the dogs in the wings, and so could Venus. A little circle of anxiety was set up, until Joy's warnings became a self-fulfilling prophecy and Venus put on a fine display of tearing Joy apart. All she really did was graze Joy's head with a paw, although the newspapers the next morning had a field day reporting that Venus had drawn blood.

On the following Saturday, with Venus again standing in for Demi, a drunk in the audience threw a balled-up napkin onto the stage, bouncing it off Venus as she posed on the mirror ball. Spooked, Venus wrapped her teeth around Joy's arm, not breaking the skin but leaving a nasty bruise. Now, if there is one thing that drives Joy insane it is strangers taking liberties with our animals. Don't touch, don't poke, don't even stand by the cage and make a pest of yourself, because Joy will be all over you. Realizing where the napkin had come from, Joy took the whip from my hand and walked directly off the stage and onto that man's table. She got in a swing or two before a couple of people from the cast took her by the arms and literally carried her away.

We had been warned before the show about this drunk, and so had the maître d', but he had chosen to do nothing. He roared down on me as the next number came on, but I opened my mouth first. "Why didn't you get that drunk out of there?" I shouted. "You knew he was there, everyone knew he was going to make trouble! What were you waiting for?"

The maître d' was spluttering, speechless with indignation. "Do you know who that man is?" he bellowed. "That man is an executive with the railroad company that *owns* this hotel!"

"Big deal," I retorted. "He nearly cost my wife her arm."

The railroad nabob was apparently too blitzed to realize what was happening, and we heard no more about Joy's attack. But it was another unpleasant incident in what was an unpleasant situation. We weren't used to being the act that failed. The only positive part of the whole debacle was the experience Herk was getting under his belt as he became accustomed to the lights, music and hustle of backstage and to walking on a leash as we strolled about the city each day, looking very Hollywood in our jeans and sunglasses. We drew crowds wherever we went, providing excellent publicity for the show where we were dying twice a night.

In the third month, as the humiliating engagement in Montreal was winding to a close, we took a chance and

ERA INOCENTE PERO NADIE LE CREYO
"POR ERROR" 3 AÑOS PRESO

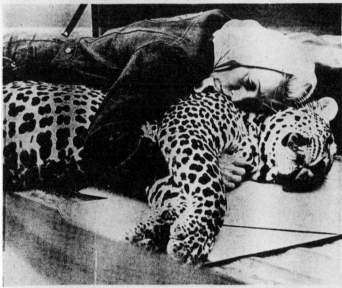

"JOY" LA DOMADORA ABRAZA A "ADONIS" EL LEOPARDO QUE AYER MURIO ENVENENADO. EL ULTIMO ADIOS A LA FIERA QUE HABIA SIDO DOMESTICADA CONVIRTIENDOSE EN UNA DE LAS PRINCIPALES ATRACCIONES DEL CIRCO DE LA PLAZA ACHO

PARA LOS AMBULANTES
HARAN 200 MERCADILLOS

Ultima Hora
EL DIARIO DE MAYOR CIRCULACION DE TODO EL PERU

DIARIO DE LAS ORGANIZACIONES DE SERVICIOS

DIRECTOR: Francisco Guerra Garcia

Boquijano 245 - Lima Telf. 279-435 276-386

Jueves, 21 de Agosto de 1975 Año XXV - N° 2685?

S/.3.50

Front page of a Lima newspaper on the day after Adonis was poisoned.

The freighter to Puerto Rico. The deadly elevator was in
the superstructure at the stern.

One of the photographs taken either just before or just
after Hercules sank his teeth into Mama's leg.

Opposite: Venus demonstrates her 20-foot leap from the mirror ball
into my arms.

The fabled photo taken by a newspaperman after I threw open the door and asked Magic if he wanted to come out of his cage.

Opposite: Joy and Hercules at ease between rehearsals at the *Festival International.*

Answering questions after a performance of *Gotta Getaway* at Radio City
Music Hall, 1984. Herk appears to be trying to give away family secrets.

Opposite: The finale kickline of *Gotta Getaway.* Joy, sixth from left,
was wearing a gold mesh dress that weighed almost as much as she did.

Joy and Demetrius during *Viva Carnaval,* at the El San Juan, Puerto Rico, before Joy became the walking wounded.

Opposite: Opening night at the *Festival International du Cirque de Montreal,* the show that ended in a much publicized sit-in.

sent our publicity package to Jack Mansell, who was putting together a new show. Joy was sure he would never meet our price, but he did, remembering us from years before. He signed us to a contract for the fall and winter in three cities—Houston, St. Louis, and Dallas.

The Houston leg of the show was at a club called "The Million Dollar City Dump," a name that left us puzzled and not a little leery until we pulled up and found it to be a perfectly respectable nightclub run by a delightful lady named Beverly Wren. She and her husband were, quite frankly, loaded—the club was his gift to her, to do with as she pleased. The name was her idea, a sort of gentle slap in the face of affectation and snobbery.

Hercules took Houston by storm, thank to Beverly Wren. She was captivated by the little tiger, and she wanted the whole world to see him. To this end she took to driving the three of us all over the city in her limousine, with Herk hanging out the window, fur ruffling in the breeze. Half the people who saw us whipped out cameras to catch the odd sight before it flew off; the other half grinned idiotically and rolled up their car windows. More than eager to share the fun, Beverly held a constant round of parties at her lavish home, inviting her wealthy friends to have their pictures taken beside their cars with Herk at their feet. He was still young enough to put up with this harmless nonsense. It was at Beverly's home that he developed his affinity for swimming pools, a luxury he has enjoyed precious little since that autumn in Texas.

Mansell's show was good. Not great, but good. There was only one mishap, a relatively minor one but one which had repercussions for many months. Catching Venus from a particularly high, long leap one evening, I stepped backwards—over the footlights, off the stage, and onto a table and chair, crushing everything beneath me. A spectator rushed forward to help and then, realizing I had a leopard in my arms, thought better of it. Neither of us was hurt, but as soon as we landed, Venus jumped back on the stage and ran to Joy's feet as if to say, "Look what Daddy did to me."

141

For two years from that day Venus would not leap. We have always encouraged her to hesitate a bit before leaving the mirror ball, to put a little suspense in her segment of the act. We can hear people in the audience whispering, "Oh, look, she's not going to do it." And then when she flies through the air, it's all the more spectacular. But there is a limit. Following the fall, she took to hesitating for a couple of minutes, crouching as if ready to go, and then suddenly squatting down and gazing about with a slighty bewildered look on her face. Now when people said, "Oh, look, she's not going to do it," she didn't. And when she did go, well, you could hardly dignify a four-inch hiccup by calling it a "leap." That part of the act became such an embarrassment that we cut it out.

Mansell was very understanding. He even paid the lighting crew and musicians overtime so that we could rehearse Venus under ideal conditions. It didn't do any good, but we appreciated the cooperation.

The show's next stop was the Barn Dinner Theatre outside St. Louis, where we were put up in apartments, which was a lot more pleasant than a motel and which fostered great camaraderie among the cast. As Christmas rolled around, the air was filled with the homey scents of baking, and everyone looked forward to the holidays with more esprit de corps than is normally found on the road.

Two girls in the show brought brownies backstage one night and offered them to Joy, who was about to go on. Joy explained that she never ate before a performance, but the girls pressed her, and finally she said, "Oh, they smell so good! I'll just take a couple for later." She knew I would probably have them for one of my unorthodox breakfasts.

I rose early the next morning, my chore for the day to get the van to a mechanic for a tuneup. I left Joy a cup of coffee by her bed and then swept through the kitchen on my way out, swilling down both brownies with coffee and starting for the door. I never made it. It was like being

142

decked from behind. My legs buckled and the floor came up and hit me in the face. Joy heard the thunk from the bedroom and rushed in to find me unconscious on the floor.

My fast-thinking wife remembered that we passed a small hospital every day en route to the dinner theater, and with the help of a couple of cast members she dragged me into the van, laid me out between the cages, and rushed down the road. The doctors immediately pumped my stomach and I came back to life. It is typical of me that my first concern was for my wig, which had come off in the van. It took the kind Oriental doctor several minutes to get me off this subject so he could tell me, through my fog, that I had ingested a tremendous amount of illegal substances and that, had our apartment not been so close to the hospital, I would now be trading in my wig for a halo and a harp.

While the doctors kept an eye on me, one of Joy's helpers from the cast went back to the apartment house to find out what was in the brownies, and returned with the news that the little Betty Crockers had used everything they could lay their hands on—grass, coke, speed, hash, a Thai stick (whatever that may be)—but they had been too stoned to stir the mess properly. I had apparently been blessed with the corner of the pan that contained the greatest concentration of unmixed ingredients, and it had nearly killed me. Joy and I do not "do" drugs in any form—our idea of a wild time is a couple of cans of light beer and a bag of Cheez-Doodles—so I was extremely susceptible.

God, I was sick. My tongue felt like thick cardboard, making talking almost impossible. I hallucinated. I sweat. I thrashed around so badly the orderlies had to tie me down. Toward evening I became relatively lucid, although my head kept going in and out on me, like a badly focused home movie. After a night's fitful sleep, I was treated to a visit by the Oriental doctor, who smiled encouragingly at me, closed the door, and made himself comfortable at my bedside. "Now," he said, laying his hands on his knees, "we're all alone. No one can hear us. Just for my own curiosity, would you tell me why you took all those drugs?"

Joy and I were reluctant, at least at this point, to implicate the two girls, although our efforts to conceal their identity proved futile because one of the orderlies picked up on what had happened and called the police. For now, I was left with the problem of explaining to this doctor that my ingestion of all that poison had been an accident. He wouldn't believe me. Over and over again he assured me that it was only curiosity that drove him to ask, and over and over again I repeated that the stuff had been baked into something I'd eaten. Finally I cried out, "Look at me! Is this the body of a druggie?"

But he just smiled. "Athletes do it. Body-builders do it. That's no answer. Now, why did *you* do it?" It was hopeless.

The two brownie-bakers got advance warning of a visit from the local police, just in time to flush their special recipes down the toilet, but Mansell found out what had happened and fired them both. Weeks later, when I was finally over my hallucinations and had calculated the full toll of damages from the hospital, I learned that one of the girls was working in Reno. I sent her a sternly worded letter to the effect that I was out $700 because of her stupidity and that the least she could do was reimburse me for my hospital and doctor expenses. Almost a year went by before she sent the money, but send it she did.

Once again, as in Puerto Rico, we had to sit through a closing show. Even if I had been able to summon the strength to perform, I didn't trust myself around the cats, whose sensitive antennae pick up distress no matter how carefully concealed. By the time we got to Dallas, a few days later, I was well enough to work, but it was several weeks before the occasional, momentary hallucinations disappeared completely.

* * *

The stage set-up at Granny's in Dallas left a lot to be desired. There was virtually no backstage at all, no room

144

for the cages. We had to dismantle Herk's cage, carry the pieces into our dressingroom, and reassemble them. Unable to find room for the other cages, we considered walking the cats to and from the stage area, but we had had too many accidents with this procedure in the past and rejected it.

After considerable trial and error we landed on a workable, if rather unpleasant solution, in which we hauled the magic cage up a series of ramps to a small platform above the stage. For our opening, I crouched uncomfortably in place behind the cage, where there was just enough room for my feet to get purchase, and then the platform, cage, cat and I were lowered to the stage floor. Once the magic cage, with Demi inside, was in place, the other cats were walked into the theater on leashes—undesirable, but there was no other way.

To get ready for all this rigmarole, we had to come into the theater an hour before it opened, which meant three hours before showtime. Since we had to walk the cats right through the dining area, it seemed only sane to get them into the theater before the audience sat down to eat. Three hours before a performance the waiters were doing their thing, setting the tables, or rather, in many cases, standing around smoking and talking and waiting until the very last minute to do what they were being paid to do. They really resented our intrusion into their nightly kaffeeklatch. Joy came through the front door with the cat and called, "Clear for the cat. Clear for the cat." All each waiter had to do was pull a table or two out of our path and then stand clear himself, but they acted as though we were asking for the moon. One evening there was a minor rebellion, one waiter standing firmly in the path.

"Clear for the cat!" Joy demanded.

The waiter shrugged. "He doesn't bother me."

From behind Joy I could almost see her hackles going up. "Did it ever occur to you," she said slowly, through a tight jaw, "that you might be bothering him?"

"He can come right through here," replied the waiter, waving a hand to indicate the suggested route.

"No, he can't," snapped my wife. "Now, move!"

The waiter stared at us. "I'm not moving," he said, flatly.

"Oh, yes, you are!" And she zapped him with the hot shot. The waiter rose visibly into the air, barking like a dog. To Joy's vanishing back he shouted that he was going to sue. "Fine," called Joy over her shoulder, "but next time, get out of the way."

The hot shot, a battery-powered wand that carries a low-voltage electric shock, is always with us when we are working with the cats. We have never used it, at least not on our animals. Its real purpose, should the worst ever happen, is to convince the animal to let go of whatever it has sunk its teeth into. Many trainers rain blows on the animal's head, with pipes or chains, but all this does is make the animal more enraged, and it bites down harder. The slight electric shock from the hot shot, as one might expect, gives just enough jolt to distract the cat and to cause a relaxation of the jaws.

For a week everything in Dallas proceeded smoothly. The audiences were marvelous, and the very talented Evans Brothers orchestra did so well with our music that we hired them to make our own click track. The waiters never did warm up to us, except for one waitress, who developed a crush on the jaguar. Every day she went out of her way to see him, and he soon began flipping over with delight at the sound of her whispered, "Hi." To this day, Joy can say, "Demi, I want a Jenny flip," and he'll roll over in exactly the same way.

And then Hercules got sick. Just before going on for the first show on New Year's Eve, we noticed that he had a lump under his jaw, and his nose was hot. We were very concerned about him but there was nothing to do but leave him in his cage and go on for the show. As always, the other animals sensed our anxiety, and Demi in particular became very distressed, rubbing his head so hard against the bars of his cage that he opened his old wound from Puerto Rico and emerged from the illusion with blood all over his face. The audience soon noticed the

146

problem and we could hear them oohing and gasping. For once, I kept my cool, handing Joy the leash and reaching down to a stage-side table for a napkin. Instead of pretending all was well, I made a mini-performance out of wiping his face, simultaneously relaxing the audience and giving them a treat.

By the time we got off the stage, the lump under Herk's jaw had grown to the size of a small grapefruit. We had a rough time finding a vet on New Year's Eve, and were making calls all over hell's half acre until a woman in the booking office remembered that a horse doctor was coming in for the second show. She managed to intercept him and he paid a call on us before joining the audience. His diagnosis: Herk had an abscessed fang.

And he was very, very sick. The vet gave us a supply of antibiotic capsules, told us to get them into him with fierce regularity throughout the night, and showed us how to wipe out the pus so that he wouldn't swallow it, since the abscess had already lanced itself. He warned that unless we were very watchful, Herk could be dead by morning.

Thank goodness all our cats are hearty eaters. The old pill-in-the-meatball trick worked, Herk got his first dose, and we went out for the second performance. The tiger gave us an excellent excuse for begging out of the champagne party after the show—we hate being anywhere except safe in our human and feline beds on this raucous holiday. The cast presented us with a bottle and helped us get the very ailing Herk into the van. By now he could no longer walk under his own steam and his body felt clammy, a very odd sensation on a furry animal's hide.

Once again, it was snowing. That winter in Dallas was so bad that the show at Granny's got snowed out six times, which has to be something of a record.

Animals were not permitted in our apartment but this was no time to consider the rules. Somehow the two of us managed to haul Herk's carcass up to the second floor; our adrenalin must have been working overtime. We laid

147

him out at the foot of our bed, stayed awake long enough to give him another pill, nursing ourselves with champagne while keeping an eye on him, until exhaustion took over and we fell asleep. It was nearly three o'clock in the morning.

Directly under our window sat the van. The long cord to its heater ran across the little parking lot, up the wall of the building, and into our window. Herk's comrades should have been safe and warm for the night, but hardly had our heads hit the pillow when there was a stomach-churning squeal of brakes, a crash, and the sound of a vehicle trying to get traction in the snow. We flew to the window in time to see a car extricating itself from the front corner of the van and attempting to pull away.

With only boots on our feet and a robe Joy grabbed, we ran into the street. I went to survey the damage while Joy tore off down the street in search of the car, feeling every vehicle along the way for one that was still warm. The door of the van was more off than on, twisted around on its own hinges, and the heater was lying face down, its cord severed.

Joy returned, unsuccessful, as I was maneuvering the door back into place, and just as another car pulled up, full of young people. "We've been following her," one of the kids shouted out the window. "She's drunk. We knew something like this was going to happen. We have her license number." They had already contacted the police.

We thanked the kids for their help, managed to get the cord reconnected to the heater, and climbed wearily back into bed. Daylight was just making an appearance when I was awakened by a loud sloshing noise. I was so delighted to find myself staring at the rear end of Hercules, who was drinking water from the commode, that I nudged Joy awake. "Look," I whispered. She raised her head a little, smiled with relief, and flopped back to sleep. Much later in the morning I woke up again, to see Herk's seemingly disembodied head watching me intently from the foot of the bed. His bright eyes seemed to be saying, "Didn't want to bother you, Dad."

"Herk," I whispered, "good to see you."

"Ffft, ffft," he replied. He was a glorious sight as he turned around and shuffled off to the bathroom to drink the bowl dry.

When we were fully awake and were sure Hercules was back on his feet, we called the vet to give a progress report. After he reminded us to keep an eye on the fang, warning that it would probably break off at some point in the future, Joy asked him to send us a bill. "Oh," he replied, "I wouldn't think of charging you for that. I was coming to the show, anyway."

Joy was delighted to see the end of the show at Granny's. "If we stick around here any longer," she intoned ominously one night, "something really awful is going to happen. I just know it." Nothing really awful happened, but she was shaken enough by the constant upheavals to miss our exit coming into St. Petersburg. She then compounded the mistake by taking the wrong road in an effort to turn around, and ended up going back across Tampa Bay, some 11 miles, before getting straightened out. Joy, the Great Navigator, lost almost within sight of her home.

Little things pile up, and make little nightmares. We decided to make a quick stop at the A&P near our home for a few essentials to stock the empty larder, and were thunderstruck to discover that in the few weeks we had been away it had closed and been replaced by another chain. Joy bowed her head on the steering wheel. "This is too much," she moaned, "when you can't even trust your supermarket to stay put." After what we had been through, the A&P's departure felt like a personal insult.

Finally our snug harbor, our house, came into view. Bone tired, we pulled the van up to the gate and called to our caretaker, Matt, who had been installed in the little apartment atop the cat castle to mind the house and grounds and to feed the dogs. There was no reply. As we fiddled around for keys to unlock the fence, the two dogs wandered into view, and the sight of them nearly destroyed us. They were all skin and bones, dragging their tails and hardly able to work up the energy to greet us. Then we noticed the garbage strewn all over the yard. One thing our dogs definitely do not do is raid garbage pails. Something was terribly, terribly wrong.

Frantically we called again for Matt, and got silence in return. When we were finally through the gate, I ran up to the apartment and was not surprised to find it deserted, everything except the larger pieces of furniture gone. Over the next few days we were filled in by our neighbors and by a friend who was in the habit of coming by now and then just to say hello to the dogs and cats. He said that Matt had decamped only three or four days before our return, after using the money we sent for dog food to throw parties in the apartment. This friend had come around one day and seen Matt throwing slices of white bread off the balcony of the apartment to the half-starved dogs below. Neighbors told of endless car-washing parties, which certainly explained the hair-raising water bill that came a few days after our return. Closer examination of the apartment revealed marijuana seeds everywhere, on the floor, under the bed, stuck in the seams and crevices of the remaining chair. He had had himself one heck of a good time. I hope for his sake I never run into him again.

Most of the chicken we had in reserve for the cats ended up inside the dogs that evening, but they ate so greedily we had to hold back for fear they would literally eat themselves into a coma. We spent that first night of our return in a blind rage, cursing the day we had ever laid eyes on Matt.

The following evening the cats were due for a bone treat, an ugly but satisfying event in which our pets undergo a sort of temporary but violent personality change, turning from lovable, cuddly friends into raging, snarling, growling beasts. All our cats are voracious eaters, but bone time is something special. The sheer size of the knucklebones is probably what reduces these animals to such a display of greed and possessiveness. Whatever the reason, I have to hide the dish behind my back when I approach the cats, because if they see the bones coming they begin to flail around in their cages with such force that they are actually in danger of doing physical damage to themselves.

On this second night back from the tour, a couple of friends dropped by after the bones had been distributed and, despite the darkness, I volunteered to take them to the cat castle for a visit. As I turned on the light, one of the guests asked me why Herk's tooth looked odd. Odd, indeed. As predicted by the vet in Dallas, the fang had split; only half of it was still in his mouth, the other half presumably having been dislodged by the knucklebone.

Our local vet, summoned in a hurry, announced that surgery was called for. A fang is really just a long, pointed extension of the jaw bone. It cannot be pulled like an ordinary tooth but rather the damaged portion must be literally chiseled away from the underlying structure. Less informed doctors have been known to attempt to yank the fang out, sending hairline fractures through the jawbone and leaving the animal to suffer such weakness in later years that eating becomes impossible. We had tremendous faith in this doctor, but we couldn't help being terrified of something going wrong. The thought that we might lose our tiger, our precious Hercules, was enough to reduce us to quivering jelly.

Hercules came through the surgery beautifully and now has a slightly crooked but rather impishly engaging three-fanged smile.

9

After a few weeks of recuperation we set out for an appearance at the Shriner's circus in Youngstown, enduring a dead battery along the way just to keep things interesting.

We were particularly exhausted on our first day at the circus, because, in addition to everything else, we had been up and about since 5:00 A.M. to tape an early-morning talk show. But since the first performance was scheduled for ten the next morning, rehearsals were in order before we could all turn in. A lighting rehearsal didn't go well at all, and Joy was despairing that our carefully planned pyrotechnics would be a shambles the next day. Then there was a tremendous ruckus with an act that tried to weasel in ahead of us for a music rehearsal, during which I lost my temper and threatened to quit. The music run-throughs didn't even start until nine in the evening, by which time the entire cast was exhausted and testy.

When the first show rolled around the next morning, we were absolutely wrung out. As always, the animals picked up on the tension and became feisty and nervous. If we and the pets had been less tired, perhaps things would have been different, but when the lights suddenly went out in the auditorium during our adagio, no member of our little ensemble was prepared to cope.

It was very dark, the only light coming from small apertures at the top of the auditorium, which was no help at all. We were sure that the blackout would be a very brief thing, so we kept going. As Joy got into the magic cage for her illusion she whispered to me, "Be careful taking Demi out to the mirror ball." When she vanished and Demi appeared in her place, it was almost impossible to find his neck in the dark and slip the collar around him. Somehow I managed and even got him up on the ball in time for Joy's reappearance. He didn't seem confused at all as she took the nylon leash from me and pointed the baton at him, cuing his sit-up. We don't call Demi "the robot" for nothing. He was in this position in a nightclub one evening when a waiter dropped a fully-loaded dinner tray over a balcony. It hit the floor with a crash that caused everyone in the place to jump four inches into the air, but Demi just swiveled his neck around a bit to give the waiter a baleful stare. Unfortunately, in Youngstown, his nerves were not what they should have been. As Joy cued him, someone suddenly opened a door leading to a bright, sunlit hallway. A wide swath of light streamed into Demi's face, startling and confusing him.

A frightened cat will normally make a mad dash for his cage, a source of security, a known quantity. But temporarily blinded and in strange surroundings, Demi instead took off for the light. Joy immediately took stock of the situation, and, realizing that the armed guards around the arena would shoot first and ask questions later, she quickly wrapped the leash in and around her fingers and resolved to hang on no matter what. This cat, she thought, is going to get away from me only at the cost of my hand.

In the course of a few seconds Demi dragged Joy about twenty-five feet, across the ring toward the hallway. She slid along on her side, sustaining terrible bruises as she hit the ring curb with a sickening thunk and bounced over it. A Shriner standing in the corridor, directly in the cat's path, told us later that he saw that pile of spotted muscles coming at him and thought, "This is it. I'm dead." But just as inexplicably as he retreated in Puerto Rico, Demi now stopped, sat down at the man's feet and looked up at him as if to say, "Have you seen my cage?"

Hard in pursuit, I reached Joy just as the house lights came on. Bending down to take the leash from her and relieve her of Demi, I was horrified to find that it had become part of her hand. I had to literally pry it out of her skin, bits of which and a great deal of blood were all over the black nylon. Together we guided Demi back to his cage, patting his head and assuring him that everything was all right, and then Joy, her bloody hand behind her back, gave the audience a deep curtsy and walked off stage. Out in the hall she encountered another Shriner, who, seeing her distress, offered to help her to her dressingroom. Frightened and angry, she insisted, "I'm all *right*! I don't *need* any help!" But after a few steps she dared to pull the hand from behind her back. She took one look at it, turned back to the Shriner in horror, wailing, "Now you can help me," and collapsed in his arms.

The ringmaster and his wife, knowing that I couldn't leave the animals to take Joy to the hospital, went in my stead, riding with her in the ambulance. Joy was calm and even asked the attendant for a beer, which of course was denied.

The first doctor who appeared pronounced her injury the "worst rope burn" he'd ever seen and began to mumble about a week in the hospital. When Joy protested that she had to get back to work immediately, he refused to treat her. "You'll probably never do another handstand," he intoned, "let alone do one tomorrow." And he left. The next man through the door was equally gloomy, and equally reluctant to attend to someone so obviously demented as to think she could resume work within twenty-four hours. Finally a good old-fashioned family physician came in, turned the hand this way and that, and said, "Yeah, it's pretty bad, but I think you'll be able to do anything you want with it."

The hand took a lot of stitches, especially the little finger, which was more bone than flesh, and a lot of butterfly bandages. Back at the circus even Joy realized that a swollen, bandaged hand was no asset to a performer, and reluctantly we told the producer we couldn't continue. He was very sympathetic, paid us for the time we had put in as well as return transportation, and wished us good luck. We were forced to hang around another six days, until the stitches came out, and then we were on our way. We were more than halfway home before Joy realized how painfully bruised she was from her collision with the ring curb.

The little finger is permanently but slightly impaired. When the two hands are held up side by side, it is obvious that the finger on the left hand is arched out and back in again, rather crescent-shaped. Joy claims it bothers her only when she types—not a serious handicap considering that when I pried her free of the leash the hand looked like chopped meat.

Joy as always had to be physically restrained from her rigorous exercise schedule, carrying on as though she was preparing for an Olympic decathlon. She had hardly got back into her routine when she struck the damaged hand against the side of the trailer, opening up some of the wounds. The woman is impossible.

10

Later in the year we returned to St. Louis, to the Plantation Dinner Theater, where the owner of St. Petersburg's equivalent, the Showboat Dinner Theatre, came upon us while previewing the show for his own place. As we negotiated with him, we kept absolutely mum about the fact that we lived not 15 miles from his establishment. Over the years we have learned that producers are very wary of "local talent." Just the fact that we made St. Petersburg our home was enough to discourage managers of places as far away as Orlando. These people apparently do not realize that everybody has to live *somewhere*.

The Showboat production, a rerun of the Plantation's show, opened in early January, just after the Christmas holidays. As we were preparing for our opening, Joy's mother arrived for a Christmas respite from the Maine winter. She is a great supporter of us and our careers but frequently remarks that while she "doesn't mind" animals, she isn't "crazy about them." She has been known to be leery of poodles. In spite of her fears she worries as

156

much as we do when one of our pets is ailing, and she has frequently helped in the training, holding a cat by the end of a leash and otherwise being closer to them physically than she probably would prefer. Antar, the short-lived black panther purchased as a backup to Aladdin, was the lone exception, but then, Antar was a very special animal.

The Showboat opening was only a day away when Mama decided it would be nice to have her picture taken with Hercules. The tiger had grown enormously and was a really big animal, nearly seven feet long and approaching 500 pounds. But he was and is of even disposition, with the regal serenity of his species. Visits inside the house were not unknown. Photographers from newspapers and magazines, enthralled by the beauty of the beast, often request pictures of us *en famille*, Herk at our feet when he was little, and then us at Herk's feet when he grew up.

I set the camera up for a picture of Mama and Hercules standing in the doorway of the livingroom. Joy was to take the pictures while I stood out of sight around a corner, holding Herk firmly on a long chain, beyond the reach of my mother-in-law but close enough to make a nice photo. Just as Joy clicked the shutter, Herk turned and reached a mighty paw toward Mama's leg. I pulled back on the chain as hard as I could, struggling to bring him under control, while Mama stood frozen in her tracks. As I pulled him into a sitting position, Joy called out, "Mama, can't you help by getting out of the way?"

Mama's face contorted with tears. "I can't," she whimpered. "He bit me."

We'll never know exactly what happened because whatever Herk did, he did it with lightning speed. We have two pictures, one showing Herk a few feet from Mama, another showing Herk reaching out with his paw. He must have sunk his three fangs into her leg just after that second picture was taken. The two of us were standing right there and saw nothing.

The wound was bad, and bleeding liberally. Hastily I doused the leg with peroxide and packed it with ice

157

wrapped in towels. As we hurried off to the hospital, we realized that things would go badly for us at the Show-boat if word got out that our tiger had bitten someone. Thus we came up with what has become known as "the fence that bit my mother." I remembered a length of wrought-iron picket fencing that was lying alongside the house, left over from who-remembers-when. It was a nasty thing, sharply pointed and rusting in the Florida climate. The three of us conspired to tell the people at the hospital that Mama had fallen on it.

We were kept waiting about nine hours at the hospital, my fault, partly, because I had done such a good job of bandaging the wounds that Mama was no longer bleed-ing. No blood, no hurry, I guess. Joy was frantic that her mother get a tetanus shot but her pleas fell on deaf ears. It was the height of the tourist season in Florida and the place was busy with the extra holiday crowd of traffic ac-cidents and other mishaps. But when she was finally treated, our story held up. It doesn't say much for our local physicians that they failed to recognize an animal bite, but, on the other hand, if it did occur to a doctor that the wounds looked like fang marks, he wouldn't be likely to stick his head out the door and ask, "I say, by the way, was this woman perhaps bitten by a tiger?"

Mama was more concerned about bad publicity than we were. She swore us to secrecy, promising that she her-self would go to her grave before she told anyone the truth about her scars.

11

In October of the year in which the fence bit Joy's mother, we got a really choice booking at the Brighton Hotel in Atlantic City. We were very excited about the prospect of a long engagement in a first-class establishment, but there were some immediate problems. There was no freight elevator, and the employees' lift was far too small for the cages, leaving the only access via a ramp in the parking garage. The overhead was too low for the van, forcing us to go through a daily routine of transferring the cages to a forklift for the ride up. Demi had been paranoid about these "mean machines" since he was so rudely dropped to the ground at the airport in Lima, and his memory did not fail him now. Fortunately for all of us, the stage manager, Dwight, was a jewel of a human being who sympathized with our problems and respected the cats' individual personalities and quirks. He did his best to smooth a path for us each day, and after a while Demi ceased his forklift-hysteria and actually seemed to take a shine to Dwight.

159

The valets who worked the garage were thoroughly annoyed by our regular disruption of their money-earning activities and over the course of our stay they developed a deep and abiding distaste for us that nothing could diminish.

A source of constant distress, especially for Joy, was the endless invective from guests watching us bring the animals in for the show. With the first performance at three in the afternoon, we had to get started around lunch time, when there were crowds of people lining the hallways around the dining rooms. As we passed by each day we were treated to volumes of ignorant nonsense about our "poor, mistreated animals," to the point where Joy was forever on the verge of exploding. This "tsk-tsking" and "tut-tutting" by people who think all animals are better off "free" drives Joy up the wall. It would have been nice, during this particularly trying time, if she could have had the following printed and handed to each of them as she struggled by each day. It was written by Gerry Durrell, founder of the Jersey Wildlife Preservation Trust, which runs one of the best conservation zoos in the world, on a tiny island off the coast of France:

Unfortunately, this attitude . . . is still rife among the well-intentioned but basically ignorant who insist on talking about Mother Nature as though she were a benevolent old lady instead of the harsh, unyielding and totally rapacious monster that she is.

But she had no such handout and instead had to rely on Dwight, who walked calmly alongside her murmuring over and over, "Now, now, Joy, control yourself."

Additional difficulties came from the location of the dressingrooms, downstairs amid the closets and carts and nameless doors of the laundry area. There were frequent and explosive encounters between the cleaning staff and the showgirls. The former regarded the latter as nothing more than fancily-clad whores and hassled them at every opportunity, making crude remarks and pinching parts of passing anatomies. From time to time

160

the maintenance men, either by choice or by accident, would leave a fully-loaded laundry cart in front of a dressingroom door for a fast-change hoofer to slam into in her rush for the stage.

And there were fires. At least a half dozen of them, over a period of about two weeks. Some dissatisfied employee, apparently seeking revenge but either unwilling or unable to start a definitive conflagration, was setting small fires in confined areas, like linen closets or refuse bins. We were in a state of constant astonishment over the man with the chimpanzee act, who locked his apes in a dressingroom each night and left, apparently unconcerned about the possibility of returning to a room full of asphyxiated or burned animals. At least at night our pets were safe. Since our contract was for such a long period of time, we rented a "farmhouse" outside of Atlantic City. The place was really a dump, but we put a lot of our spare time into it and left it looking far better than when we found it. And the animals were in their trailer right outside the door, far from any potential disaster at the Brighton.

With the exception of Radio City Music Hall, the Brighton provided the best crew we have ever worked with. All of them ran their fannies off for us and went out of their way to counter the problems we were having on other fronts. As is our custom, we sought each of them out at the end of the first week for a well deserved tip, but they refused the extra money, then and for the rest of our stay. We were finally able to express our gratitude when the show closed, by buying the nicest personal gifts we could find for each of them, from warm winter jackets to leather briefcases. We thoroughly enjoyed buying those presents.

Once the rash of fires came to a halt, and we got into a routine of dealing with the garage and the dressingrooms, things settled down. By mid-December we were relaxed and comfortable, mentally set for a long residence in New Jersey. And then came a crushing blow. The Brighton had been sold, to become the Sands, and the entire show was to be dismantled at the end of the year. Instead of twelve months of guaranteed income, we would be out of work after less than three months. Part of the disappointment was having to give up a very rare working relationship with a producer who appreciated us for what we were. Unlike others in our experience, Si Zentner didn't see Joy as a threat to the stage presence of his "girls," he didn't regard our animals as a nuisance, he didn't ask more of us than he was paying for—he was a pleasure to work with.

Christmas Day was a sad affair. We had expected to spend it in a celebration with our fellow performers and friends from the crew and hotel but instead we passed the time packing away the bits and pieces of equipment that were cluttering our dressingroom. We had less than a week left, since the last show of the year was not to be ours but a special appearance by Carol Channing. Her visit to our dressingroom, where she enthused over our act and praised my costumes to the stars, was a great boost on what was otherwise a very depressing occasion.

12

When we were able to get a major booking at the Flamingo Hilton in Las Vegas, we felt that our dreams had come true. Fond memories of our adagio days there, before it had become part of the Hilton chain, led us to believe that we were in for some good times, excellent money, enthusiastic audiences and prize working conditions. During the 1960s we had appeared there in support of Norm Crosby and Bob Goulet. We had had the time of our lives. Once we had broken into the animal-act world, we had set our sights on a comeback, dreaming of the money we would make and the fun we would have.

The agent who set up the Las Vegas booking for us—we'll call her Michelle—was in constant contact with us before we left St. Petersburg. At first we were grateful for her attentiveness, advising her what sort of place to look for as a rental home during our stay, giving her our lighting and music requirements. But after weeks of nightly long-distance calls from her California office, usually timed just as we were putting the cats in for the night, we began to weary of her attention. Joy felt like telling her that the contract entitled her to ten percent but not the right to tie us up on the telephone for two hours every night.

One of Michelle's most urgent calls questioned how much room we needed for the act. She thought the stage would provide an area about 30 feet long by about 12 feet deep. "That's a little tight," I said, "but we can manage if we have to." She was mumbling something about a "platform," but I couldn't pin her down, and I kept getting the feeling there was something she wasn't telling me. She was so glib, but also so oblique. Our act requires a high ceiling, a large stage, quality lighting effects, good music, and a quick and competent stage crew. In my nightly conversations with Michelle, I began to get the uncomfortable feeling that the Flamingo Hilton was unwilling or unable to provide the support we needed.

Our departure from St. Petersburg was not auspicious. Only an hour or so from home an axle snapped on the trailer, leaving us to limp back to the house after a hasty patch job with 2x4's. We couldn't go back to our own beds because, anticipating a lengthy absence, we were having the place fumigated against Florida's persistent bug population. Our good friends Dan and Amy Schramek, seeing us heading for a motel, insisted on putting us up for the two or three days required to repair the trailer. Two axles and four tires later, and a good deal poorer, we set out again. Joy the planner/navigator always leaves plenty of extra time for mishaps on long trips, so we weren't concerned. We could still reach Las Vegas on schedule.

But whatever gremlins there are who bless people on highways weren't done with us yet. Outside Dothan, Alabama, in the middle of nowhere on a Saturday evening, the clutch on the van went out. Somehow we got into Dothan and pulled up to a chain auto-parts store. The three employees fiddled around with the van a bit and then announced that, because the van was so old, the tiny part causing the trouble was irreplaceable. Now we were getting upset, with Joy on the verge of tears, seeing our long-awaited contract in Las Vegas going up in smoke.

Finally, as the store was closing for the night, one of the young men mentioned that his brother was a mechanic and he would "try to get him out here." We watched him lock up the shop and then sat in the gathering twilight, feeling very helpless and alone, and thoroughly convinced that no one would ever arrive to help us. We were very surprised when a car suddenly pulled up, disgorging the employee's brother who, with his wife and small son, was dressed up to have a family picture taken at Sears before the store closed at 9 P.M. Their name was Evans.

Mr. Evans took off his jacket and, oblivious to the dirt, got on the ground and began poking around under the van. Hours passed, during which he occasionally sent his wife back home for a tool and we amused his son by showing him the animals. Not once did any member of the family ever voice a complaint about the loss of their evening. When Joy broke down and cried in frustration, Mrs. Evans put her arms around her and offered what comfort she could. "I know it's easy for me to say don't worry, so I won't say that. And for me to say don't cry, so I won't say that. But I want you to know that I believe the good Lord meant us to help you, and there is no way we're going to abandon you. Trust me." Joy was so touched by this display of warmth and kindness from a stranger that she cried all the harder.

About two o'clock in the morning Mr. Evans announced that the part needed welding, which would have to wait until the following day. Still full of energy, he drove off to get his father's big tow truck and returned to pull us to a nearby motel for the night. He promised to be back in the morning, first thing after church. Exhausted and anxious, we fell into a deep sleep, with the cats safely moored right outside our door, where Mr. Evans had gently placed the van.

It was scarcely nine in the morning when the whole family returned, having not only attended church but also visited the welder. Another three hours of labor went by while the repaired part was put back where it belonged. There was one, odd wire left over, just sort of hanging there, and Mr. Evans remarked, "Well, I don't know what this is, or where it goes, but I do guarantee this van will get you to Las Vegas."

I took Joy aside by the elbow and whispered, "How much money do we have left to play with?"

"I don't know," she croaked, "something under two hundred dollars."

I gathered up $150 and offered it to Mr. Evans, who looked truly shocked. "Oh, no," he said. "The welder charged me twenty dollars, and I have to give my father thirty for the towing, but I can't take any money from you." He was most adamant.

Finally I gave it to the little boy, saying "Give this to your father later, after we're gone." The child looked hopefully up at his mother, who gave a quiet nod of approval.

We will never forget the Evans family. Many, many people have helped us on the road and we are forever grateful to them, but the Evanses were something truly special.

Around dinner time that night, along the Mississippi, we were looking for a place to stay when a trooper appeared behind us, "bubblegum machine" flashing. We knew we couldn't be speeding—on a good stretch we're lucky to cruise at 50 miles per hour, hauling all that equipment. The trooper politely informed us that the lights on our trailer were not working, and in unison we crowed, "There's the missing wire!"

We shook off the gremlins, probably when we crossed Old Man River, and made it to Las Vegas without further trauma, although the van labored terribly over the mountains and there were moments when we had visions of losing power altogether and rolling backward into the prairie.

The rental house selected for us was owned by a Mr. Clarke, who was the very incarnation of Kentucky Fried Chicken's Colonel Sanders, white from his hair to his shoes, with a Cadillac to match. His modern home, on a cul-de-sac in a nice neighborhood, was surrounded by an eight-foot wall, which suited our needs precisely. We had to lay down first and last months' rent as well as a month's security, which came to $3,000, including lawyer's fee, but we were getting a lot for our money.

Mr. Clarke brought the papers to us for signing, which is when Joy pointed out that we couldn't live with a requirement of three months' notice to break the lease. "We have one-month options at the hotel," she told him. "No problem," he replied, and crossed out the paragraph. Joy also noticed that the address of the "rented property" was not the address of the house, to which Clarke said, "Oh, that's the other house I rent. I'm always getting them mixed up." And he crossed out the address. He seemed so nice and trustworthy, offering to lend us his car so we could run around making arrangements for water, electricity and the like. We were supposed to have ten days for all this nonsense, but the breakdowns in Florida and Alabama had cut that window to less than a week.

While we had put a lot of money into our costumes and equipment, it was our beat-up van that made the first impression. About eight slow-moving young men met us at the dock of the hotel; some of them appeared to be either drunk or doped. They stood around with their hands in their pockets while we parked, and then one asked, "How do you unload that thing?" Joy leaped to the ground and said brightly, "Like this," and whipped out the ramp . . . which no longer fit. The replacement of the axles in Florida had altered the height of the van. For a few seconds there was terrible silence. We had confirmed their suspicions; we didn't know what we were doing. And they were rough! They must have all been trained by the Bash & Dent Brothers Moving Company. Our equipment was yanked, pulled, tossed, pushed, all without any consideration for fragility. We watched the unloading in grim silence, fingers crossed behind our backs.

When I saw the stage we were supposed to be working on, I nearly fainted. Not anything near 12 feet by 30, it was a three-foot-wide plywood platform wedged between two side stages, in front of a curtain. We were expected to perform adagio dancing and illusions and Venus's 20-foot leap in an area the size of a bathtub! When I tried to crouch behind the cage, my usual opening position, I couldn't get enough purchase in the three inches left for me. Once out from behind the cage, there wasn't enough room for me to crack the whip without scalping people in the first row. Joy couldn't do a handstand on my arm without entangling one leg in the curtain. And so on. The stage manager, with whom we had worked in Guy Lombardo's Jones Beach production, explained that a "plug," a portable extension behind the curtain, would be locked into place as we began our performance, but advised us to pace the first part slowly, to give the crew time to perform the installation. The reason for this limited space, and the plug, was that this particular extravaganza included a very unusual feature, an ice show. Without the plug we were in danger of falling off the narrow stage, through the curtain, onto solid ice.

The producer had told us our act needed "Vegasizing," whatever that meant. More glitter, apparently, although we already had so much spangle and jangle on our costumes we were in danger of tipping over from the weight. As I looked at the disastrous performing area, I said to the stage manager, "Is this what you guys mean by 'Vegasizing'? Didn't you see our videotape? You're going to destroy us!"

"Don't worry," he grumbled, "we'll fix it."

There was only one solution: Alter and adapt our act to fit the circumstances. We went furiously to work, because opening night was only three days away. Making changes to a routine that was by now second-nature to us required a 'round-the-clock effort. I was in a rage with frustration and anxiety, but Joy remained calm, and with her patience and guidance we worked out solutions to all the problems, making the best use possible of the two side stages. On one occasion we went to work at ten in the morning and continued so intensely that as we started out of the building I was surprised to see that it was only four o'clock. Joy remained mute as I babbled away about how well we'd done in only six hours and then, as I stared dumbly at the dark city streets, said, "Yes, Ron, it's four o'clock—in the morning!"

Opening night of "City Lites" was a spectacular success. Audience response to the show, including us, was marvelous. Our dressingroom was crammed with flowers and telegrams sent from all over the country.

But things refused to settle down. In this modern-day Sodom-and-Gomorrah-in-the-Desert, we were constantly caught between the producer, who kept telling us to "tighten up" the performance ("It doesn't work well when it's loose") and the stage manager, who reminded us every day to take our time so that the plug could be put into place. These two pieces of conflicting advice made it impossible for us to know where we stood, and there were performances where all we could do was tell the maestro to watch us and see what we were including and what we were omitting. The whole thing made for very unsettled working conditions, to say the least.

The last straw came on the second occasion that the crew tripped the device which produces Hercules' "magic" appearance under Joy after she descends from the levitation. Over and over we warned the crew that in moving the cage around they had to be extra careful not to touch the two pins that control this delicate mechanism. There is nothing more disheartening than looking over in the middle of a levitation and seeing the cage in its corner with the curtain half off, revealing parts of the tiger's anatomy. The illusion becomes a travesty.

In the second month our agent, who had been invisible through our tribulations with the stage crew, suddenly appeared. Her timing was marvelous. She came fluttering up to us just before a show to say that the producer wasn't happy and was considering not picking up our option. Questioned about where the problems lay, she became her usual vague self, mentioning specifically only that there was displeasure over our closing, which we gathered was not considered a "strong finish" for Vegas.

We agreed to cut out the hat bit. I pointed out that, the producer's opinion notwithstanding, the audiences were eating us up. Michelle fluttered away, only to return after the second show smiling and waving and calling, "It's all fixed, everything's fine. Your option is being picked up." We still don't know what really happened that night.

Positive response to us came not only from the audience but also from the Mogul himself, Baron Hilton. Our brief encounter with him was the result of Joy's aversion to shabby treatment. It is a tradition in Vegas, albeit a distasteful one, that with the exception of opening night, acts are not invited to cast parties. But when one of these affairs was held right outside our door one night, attended by the Baron, Joy couldn't restrain herself. "I've just got to see what a real billionnaire looks like," she enthused, "and I don't care what anybody says, I'm going out there." She was picking her way through the crowd when suddenly there he was, asking, "Aren't you the lady with the tiger? Please allow me the honor of kissing your hand." And he lifted her fingers to his lips. Joy floated ten feet off the floor for days afterward.

I was on my way to get a cup of coffee between shows one evening and, passing through the crowd in the mammoth, mirror-lined casino, I suddenly saw what had to be doubles of Joy's mother and two sisters. They were half-facing me through a throng of people. I took a step or two closer, staring, not believing my eyes, and then they gave themselves away by trying to turn their backs on me, only to have their faces fully revealed in the mirror.

Mama and Beatrice and Theresa had read between the lines of Joy's letters and suspected that our lifelong dream was not panning out as expected. So they had somehow dredged up the airfare and flown out from Maine to give us a boost. They begged me not to spoil the surprise for Joy. They had tickets for the midnight show and I promised to keep their secret until they could come backstage—no easy feat, because I can't keep anything from Joy, especially when it comes to her family. But we were all familiar with Joy's self-imposed standards

170

about pleasing Mama. If she knew her mother was in the audience, she would definitely "mess up."

For the rest of the between-the-shows break I had a hard time. "I don't know why I'm so nervous tonight," I kept saying, knowing fully well why. When someone telephoned backstage to tell me where the family would be sitting, I managed to babble to Joy that "some people from Maine are in Vegas, somebody who knows your sister . . . no big deal."

We did an extra fine performance that night. Knowing approximately where the family was sitting, I was aware of their applause, but neither of us could see them over the footlights. As we left the stage, Joy said, "Boy, did you hear all that clapping and shouting from those people from Maine? They really know how to show appreciation. I did the whole act just for them!"

Almost at once we were back on stage, our names announced to take a bow following the big "City Lites" production number. "And now, the stars of our show, Ron and Joy Holiday." The Maine contingent was on its feet as we stepped up-stage but now some of the houselights were up and beside me Joy suddenly leaned forward, her face contorted with bewilderment. The music played, "City Lites, da da de dum, City Lites . . . " and then Joy did the most unprofessional thing she's ever done in her life. Overcome with astonishment, she blurted her sister's name right out into the audience: "BEATRICE!!"

There was a joyful, tearful reunion in the dressing-room, with Joy repeating over and over, "What are you *doing* here?"

Mama and Beatrice and Theresa spent three days in Vegas, and on the assumption that they would never return, they saw everything. Theresa catnapped now and then, but the other two literally went without sleep the entire time. On their last night we stayed up talking until almost four in the morning, promised to see them to the airport the next day, and then went back to our rented house to sleep.

Very early in the morning, only an hour or two after we had turned in but long before we had to get up, there was

171

a violent pounding on the door. Joy got up to answer it, looked through the peephole, and saw three uniformed policemen, one of whom was holding a long stick with a noose on the end, the sort of thing Floridians recognize as a tool used by alligator hunters. When she opened the door the trio burst into the room, waving the stick at our half-grown dog, Bear, and yelling, "Keep him back! Keep him back!"

"What is this all about?" Joy cried.

"You've got wild animals here, lady!" one of them shouted as they looked frantically around.

"Not in the house!" my wife protested.

Once convinced that nothing was going to leap out at them from darkened doorways, the police calmed down. We were in violation of local ordinances. "Surely," Joy suggested, "it isn't a problem for a few months. We've got an eight-foot wall, nobody can even see the animals. And our landlord never mentioned any problem."

Our presence in a residential area was very much a problem, and we were ordered to move, although the officers did tell us they would give us whatever time we needed to find another place.

Toward evening of the following day we heard about a ranch for rent outside the city. The place proved perfect, with three private acres at less rent than we were paying for Clarke's house. That fine gentleman, when asked for the return of our deposit, denied ever agreeing to one month's notice. Our hands were tied because, trusting fools that we are, we had deleted the paragraph only on our copy of the lease. We had forked out a full month's rent only a day or two before our eviction, so Clarke came away with a bundle of our money. Colonel Sanders, indeed.

Moving day was awful. With no time off, we had to pack, move, and unpack all in one day, and when show-time rolled around we and the pets were shot. Venus in particular felt the strain; the tension must have been coming off us like laser beams. That night she refused to leap, and for the rest of our stay she performed erratically, jumping nicely one night, not at all the next.

172

When the letter arrived in early December, terminating our contract with the Flamingo Hilton, we were dumfounded. Management did extend us through January, which was an extra month over the current option, but this was very little consolation. In twenty-three years in the business, this was the first time we had ever been given notice. And we were devastated.

I took the letter and marched straight to the Vegas Hilton to see the producer. "Level with me," I said. "If you have one shred of honesty in you, you'll tell me what is going on."

The producer's shoulders sagged. "I don't know, Ron," he said. "It was just a bad booking, it's not working out. The Hiltons aren't happy, we're having all sorts of problems, we've got Siegfried and Roy right down the street. . . ."

Ah hah! I thought. So that's it: the competition. When we arrived in Vegas, Siegfried and Roy were putting together an all new and very spectacular show, which opened a week after we did. Someone, somewhere, didn't like the idea of two so similar animal acts running simultaneously, and since that daring duo has tremendous influence in the city, we got the shaft. The fact that we played to full houses every night, and frequently had standing ovations, didn't seem to mean anything. We were on the street.

The old van was in such bad shape that we didn't dare load it down for the trip back over the mountains, so we rented a truck to carry most of the weight. Sitting at the wheel of this monstrous and time-worn vehicle, Joy couldn't even see the trailer hitched behind but simply had to trust that it was back there, somewhere. I took over as driver of the van, carrying only the caged animals and a dog or two. The trip was an ordeal for both of us—Joy from the constant struggle to control the rented heap, which lacked even power steering, and I from my unaccustomed role as driver (on the trip west I had been behind the wheel perhaps all of two hours).

Among its other shortcomings, the rented truck had poor shock absorbers. Every bump in the road was an ad-

173

venture for Joy and her constant passenger, our shepherd pup, Bear. From my position in the lead, I had a splendid and hilarious view in my mirror: One second the two of them would be smiling and waving to me, Bear only a disembodied face over the dashboard, and the next Joy's head would vanish toward the ceiling and Bear would disappear altogether. Then Joy would bounce down, Bear would climb back up, and the whole scene would be repeated at the next flaw in the highway.

Crawling along with our load at a top speed of 50 miles per hour under the best of conditions, we were lucky to make 400 miles a day. Route 10 stretches across the widest part of Texas, turning that state into a three-day affair. Near Houston we began about 7 P.M. to watch for a place to spend the night but the raggedy motels we finally stumbled on were full of workers from the oil rigs and we had to go another 90 miles before finding a comfortable place with turn-around room and a vacancy.

The usual "no pets in rooms" sign was up, but it was chilly in Texas in January and we were very reluctant to leave the dogs out overnight. While one of us distracted the desk clerk, the other smuggled the pets up the nearby staircase to our second-story room: Pepe, then Sinbad, then Bear. The dogs knew enough to be quiet, but once in the room Pepe went into one of his chatter jags, yelling "Hi! How are ya?" at the top of his lungs, until we heard a voice in the hallway bleating, "Whose kids are making all that noise?" We quickly threw the cover over Pepe's cage, and he shut up.

Our shepherd Diamond was on her last legs by this time, old and infirm and reluctant to take one more step than was absolutely necessary. We agreed she would be better off if we didn't try to move her from the van, but when I went to give the cats their knucklebone snacks for the night I couldn't stand the sight of her big, brown eyes staring up at me. With tremendous difficulty I managed to lift and carry her to our room.

It is hard to describe how much the Vegas booking meant to us, and how bad we felt about being given notice. To say it was the disappointment of a lifetime doesn't begin to cover it. Gloom and depression were our constant companions in the month that followed, and our self-esteem took a terrible beating. We normally "withdraw" after a long period on the road, to give ourselves time to decompress and the animals a chance to relax. For a week or two we do no practice sessions and require the animals to do nothing more than sleep, eat and get fat and lazy. But after the Flamingo we saw no one and did nothing for weeks on end.

13

T he highly depressing experience in Las Vegas hung around us like a black cloud. The death of a dream is a very difficult thing to live with. At times like these it is comforting to pause and reflect where we've been and where we might be going, to look at the many mementoes of our successes scattered about the house, hanging on walls, standing on tables, filling album after album with pictures from our shows, paintings and animal statuettes given to us by friends long gone but well remembered. And we have plenty to smile about. While the constant "accidents" with our equipment in Las Vegas were not funny in the least, over the last 15 years there have been many mishaps which caused us at the time to say to each other, "Some day we'll look back on this and laugh."

Joy's costumes, for example. She has emerged from the illusion in various stages of disrepair, including the memorable time there was a toeshoe hanging from her hair. She bent over once for a bow and the bottom half of her bikini fell open, and on another occasion she reached into the wings for a mike and heard the stagehand whisper hoarsely, "Joy, your nipple is sticking out." Then there was the day she stepped out of the magic cage in her black bikini with a little crop of lamb's wool from her toeshoe clinging to her crotch, an incident she puts at the top of her list of embarrassing moments.

Just before we go on, we always check the magic compartment of the cage to be sure the pre-set cat hasn't relieved himself, but in the dark of the wings it isn't always easy to see clearly into the nether reaches of a black cage. Joy and Demi trade places in literally three seconds, so Joy has no chance to change her mind once the illusion begins. If there is a puddle in her compartment, so be it. I had to laugh one night in Vegas when there was an audible splash as she disappeared, followed by muffled curses, but while I rolled the cage into position I heard, "Go ahead, laugh. You're going to be sorry when I get out of here." And I was, because when I lifted her into the air, with the back of her costume wringing wet and her hair plastered to her head, Demi's urine dripped all over me. At times like this all we can do is hope the audience thinks we're sweating from the stagelights, and be grateful they can't smell us.

We had to reconstruct the magic cage after it fell apart during a performance. I had thoughtlessly put only one supporting bar across the underside, and after years of stress it gave out. I heard a noise but, unable to place it, began my usual course of rolling the cage across the floor, unaware that I was dragging my wife along on her rear end.

One of the most embarrassing accidents happened at the posh Chateau Frontenac in Quebec City, during our adagio days. The winter carnival was on and we were having a marvelous time when our agent, Buddy Morra, suggested that he invite the woman who did the booking for the prestigious Queen Elizabeth Hotel in Montreal to see our act, with an eye toward a contract. We had had such an arrangement with the QE once before but had been forced to cancel because of an offer from Radio City.

How we relished the chance to perform for their agent, because in 1963 the QE was a mecca for dance teams, attracting fantastic audiences and showering prestige on anyone lucky enough to work there. Our agent made the phone call and the lady from the QE said she would come, but she couldn't say when.

The Chateau Frontenac was jammed with guests but we asked the maître d' not to seat anyone behind us because theater in the round forced us to make alterations in our performance. But money changed hands and when we arrived on stage one night we found people sitting all around us. We did the best we could and probably would have pulled it off had my pants not ripped from front to back, waistband to waistband, while I was lifting Joy over my head. With a good many people behind us, there was nowhere to hide, and so I kept going, with my shirt-tails hanging out along with a good portion of my anatomy.

Life being what it is, the booking agent from the Queen Elizabeth was not only in the audience that night; she was also one of the people who were treated to the rear view. But unlike Fred Harris, who forgave us raveling toeshoe ribbons and belligerent microphones, this woman was furious. Asked how she liked our act, she hauled herself up to her full height and blasted, "All I could see was your beHIND!" She was thoroughly turned off, even by a behind as nice as mine, and never did hire us.

There is room for error everywhere. Outdoor shows in particular seem to provide tremendous opportunities for mistakes and miscalculations. A strong wind, for example, can take the fire during the "cremation" and force it back down into the mirror ball. On at least one occasion Joy emerged with the tips of her hair singed. A wet stage is a terrible hazard during the adagio, and also makes the use of electricity for the revolving mirror balls very dangerous.

When things go wrong with the cats, we can often pretend that the problem is part of the act. With such independent creatures as ours, it is usually easier to do what the cat wants than to fight him, especially on stage. Magic, for example, never hurries. He is still in the training process, learning to sit up and "kiss," and ride on my shoulders (although if he gets any bigger he may end up carrying me around). Part of his limited appearance involves nothing more than walking with me back to his cage at the far left corner of the stage, and stepping in. At first I tried to encourage him to quicken his leisurely pace, as he stepped painfully slowly along, gazing around at the audience with the curiosity of the young. But I rapidly learned that it was easier on my nerves, and amusing to the audience, if I made fun of him, saying, "Take your time, Magic. Don't hurry. That's a boy, take it easy."

Hercules likes to paw at Joy when she puts him into his sit-up. To the audience this must seem a ferocious act, but in truth he is merely reaching out to his "mother," or just wants to play with the glitter on her costume. And when he is supposed to be sitting regally at Joy's feet atop the revolving mirror ball, he often reduces himself to a pussycat by trying to "catch" the spinning light reflections that bounce off the ball in all directions.

As in every field of endeavor, lack of communication can be the cause of really big headaches. Producers misunderstand our requirements, stagehands miss their cues, musicians . . . ah, musicians. We have had some wonderful moments with them. We were booked to do our adagio at a little place on an army base in New Jersey for a one-nighter, or "club date," and went through agonies during the rehearsals, to make the musicians understand our charts. We did a trying and very thorough "talk-over," with Joy explaining each passage. The musicians didn't have much to say; we trusted that their silence signaled understanding. But when we stepped out on the stage for our actual performance, Joy made a croaking noise and said, "My God, Ron, look, they're white!" We had rehearsed four *black* musicians. They struggled with our music for a few bars, making the most awful noise, until finally Joy hissed from the stage, "Play anything, dammit! Play 28 choruses of 'Deep Purple'!" Immediately, we lost the audience, who overheard this outburst. The musicians were veterans, and right or wrong they were sacred.

We had another go-around with musicians in Florida, preparing for the same show which followed Aladdin's remarkable shit-skating performance for Victor Borge. We had a talk-over with those musicians, too, a very detailed one, and they were really enthusiastic, saying "Hey, wow, man, great charts," and the like. Joy went out of her way to point out that the words "Cut when girl splits" do not refer to her splitlike handstand on my forearm but to the actual split to the floor, which I throw her into. "Not there," she warned them, "but when I come down to the floor." Heads nodded. We went into rehearsal. I held Joy over my head, we did the double drop, she landed on the floor. But the trumpet player hung onto the note forever. We tried to signal to him that this was the place but he wasn't looking at us. He was, however, turning a lovely shade of blue. Finally Joy yelled, "CUT!" Everything came to a stop. "Why didn't you stop?" she asked.

One musician replied, "Man, you got it right here in black and white: 'Cut when girl splits.' Well, she hasn't left the stage yet!"

The only time I ever dropped Joy was while doing a "double," working two places in the same evening. At the second club, the ceiling was hung so low with lights that during the lifts Joy could feel their heat. The lights went out just as I released her from over my head into the double drop, and in the total blackness I couldn't find her wrists to break her fall. She fell past me, hitting the floor with a terrible thud which fortunately sounded a lot worse than it felt.

At Grossinger's, one of our frequent haunts, we always worked in the playhouse, but we knew that if we could adapt our act to the nightclub we would enjoy even more bookings at this mammoth hotel. Unfortunately, the ceiling in the club consisted of a series of strung-together arches, covered with acoustical tile. When we finally got a chance to perform there, I found that only the highest point of each arch provided enough room for our lifts, forcing me to maneuver very carefully into position before putting Joy over my head. But leave it to a low ceiling to generate high comedy: When I threw her into the air, her head went right through the tile. She hung there for a split second, and then came down from her own weight, bringing a good deal of the acoustical tile with her. On return visits to Grossinger's over the next few years, we always went into the club to see if the hole in the ceiling had been fixed. It probably disappeared only when Grossinger's was leveled in the fall of 1986.

14

Our first major booking after the catastrophe in Las Vegas was at a family-style animal park. We almost didn't take it, because the agent was so vague about the details. The first telephone call only inquired whether we were available. This was followed by the usual rounds of negotiation over money, which seemed meager to us until we finally found out that the park, Aqualand, was in Bar Harbor, Maine, practically a stone's throw from our families. If the agent had told us the location at the outset, the whole process could have been severely shortened.

Contract signed, sealed and delivered, Joy announced that she simply had to make a trial run in the *Entreprise*, which had just been delivered. We had been given detailed, verbal instructions about hitching it up, but we felt the lack of hands-on experience immediately. As soon as the leviathan left the driveway, it noisily unhitched itself. We put it together again, and Joy and a friend went off to some shopping. Backing into the yard on her return, she managed to demolish a YIELD sign and take out a good bit of the corner of a tolerant neighbor's lawn. Not bad for a first time out.

Loading up was a pleasure. I all but danced with glee as the winch hauled Hercules and his cage up the ramp. The expression of puzzled worry on the tiger's face had me doubled over with laughter. He stood stock-still as the cage slowly rose toward the belly of the van, but he kept one eye on me as he went, as if to say, "I hope you know what you're doing."

We were whizzing along at our usual breakneck speed of 50 mph on I-95 in Virginia when we heard the first BANG of a tire blowing. At the wheel, Joy started into the air and yelped, "Was that us?" But it was only a southbound semi. When the second BANG retorted, only a few miles up the road, I was sure it was yet another passing truck, but almost at once Joy said she could feel something wrong and she pulled over.

There was indeed a blown tire on the *Enterprise.* I stood guard on the pets and property while Joy set off on foot for a nearby exit, carrying a scrap of paper scribbled with every word and number from the blown tire. She had to hit three places before she found someone willing and able to replace such a large tire. In the process of repair we received a bit of very annoying news: The bolts that mounted the axles were in backwards. This had been no problem when the rig was empty but now, with the extra weight, the bolts were being forced against the tires. Moreover, the builder had put truck tires on the rig, instead of trailer tires. "You got a new tire, lady," the repairman said, "but you still got a problem."

The "problem" recurred only minutes later, when another tire blew, and the smoke coming from the new tire told us it wouldn't last long, either. We managed to limp a dozen miles to a place that was able to handle the monumental reworking of the axles that was now a necessity, and we were furious. Joy got on the telephone to the man who had dealt with the body works and informed him that we were going to be out almost one thousand dollars (in cash, of course) and that it was his responsibility to contact the builder and arrange for our reimbursement. The money was waiting for us when we got to Maine. After our anger subsided, we remembered the near-disaster outside of Valdosta years before and counted ourselves lucky that all we lost was time.

Notwithstanding our adventures with the *Enterprise*, we got to Maine in plenty of time to start looking for Aqualand. We had to ask a lot of directions to find it, and when we finally stumbled on it, almost by accident, we were horrified. The sign told us all we needed to know. It was a time-worn, faded wooden thing, on which our appearance had been added by hand. Sea World it was not. It looked like it hadn't earned a dime in a hundred years. When we saw the cramped, smelly quarters of the animals on the other side of the gate, only our desire to perform so close to home, and the fact that we had really been looking forward to this appearance, prevented us from heading straight back to St. Petersburg.

The sole occupant proved to be the manager of the gift shop, a really nice man who showed us where we needed to put the rig. Joy went through the most agonizing manipulations to get into position, and when we were finally in place she looked back toward the gate and announced, "There is no way I'm going to get out of here at the end of the summer." We decided to cross that bridge when we had to.

As always, Joy wanted to call her mother and tell her we'd arrived safely, and the gift-shop manager offered the use of his phone. As he stood fiddling at his desk, Joy reached her mother. "Hi, Mom, we're here. Oh, yes, wonderful. Hmm hmm, really nice place. Oh, that would be nice. No, no problems. I'll call you again before we leave. Bye." Then she thanked the manager for the use of the phone and rushed back to me at the rig. "Ron," she gasped, "I've just got to get into town and call her again. She wants to send some of her guests here on their way back to Canada. Ron, I'd *die* if any of those people saw us in this place!"

Quickly we unhitched the rig and then Joy took the pickup truck and tore off into Bar Harbor. Her mother was surprised. "Wow, two calls in one day. I guess you. . . ."

"Ma!" Joy interrupted. "The place is a *dump!* Please, don't send anybody to see us here. It's *awful!*"

Awful wasn't really the right word. Aqualand was a disgrace. On the first morning I went in search of water, to hose down the pets, cages and rig, and to fill the drinking dishes. The park manager, a young woman, sent me to a tap on a nearby hill. I attached our hose and turned on the faucet, and received a thin trickle of water. No pressure at all. "Hey," I yelled back down to the manager, "what is this?"

She smiled and waved and called back, "You're lucky to get that. We never have any pressure. It takes forever to fill the water dishes in this place."

That's when I got mad. I stormed back down the hill. "That's it!" I yelled. "Get the owner on the phone. Shake a leg! We're packing up! We're leaving!" The owner, reached at his other park elsewhere in the state, got an earful about my complaints. "This is the sort of place the organizations I belong to close down!" I told him. "Unless you do something about the living conditions of the animals, we're getting the hell out of here!"

The plumbers arrived that very day. No corners were skipped—even a new pump was installed. By that afternoon we had enough water to clean and irrigate half the state. The park manager was grateful; I had accomplished in one day what she'd been struggling with for months.

With that problem solved, I returned to the park manager and asked about the stage. "There it is," she said, pointing to a pile of lumber. The bleachers were in the same condition. The owner of the park had come to the ridiculous conclusion that I would help with the construction. I am not a carpenter. I raised my voice again, informing anyone within earshot that we needed set-up and practice time, and to get *going!*

While we waited for the stage to be built, we took a leisurely tour of the place and were disgusted by what we saw. Most of the animals had little or no shelter from the sun and rain. Water dishes were empty everywhere. It was obvious that the park manager, while well-intentioned, knew almost nothing about the care and feeding of wild animals. A cougar who did have shelter refused to come out of it because some fool at the local SPCA had advised the park to lay down pebbles as a flooring; blotches of dried blood bore witness to the condition of the pads on her paws.

The park manager also seemed to lack the aggressiveness to demand even the most basic requisites from the owner. When she failed to obtain a covering for the monkeys, after I complained that the nursing female should not be sitting in the blaring sun all afternoon, I simply took over. With the stage finished, I liberated a piece of leftover plywood and quickly constructed a cover for the cage. From then on, every time I passed by, the monkey and her baby were under the shelter.

Most of the animals were mean, and justifiably so. A baboon reacted to visitors as though he would be delighted to tear them apart, and Dandy the lioness was as hostile a cat as I'd ever seen.

Joy and I began a summer-long, sometimes quiet, often noisy campaign to educate the manager of Aqualand. We began by asking why there was rarely any water in the animals' cages. At the marmoset cage, which contained about a half dozen monkeys, water was supplied by a couple of bottles of the sort normally found in hamster cages. "I don't understand it," the park manager whined. "I keep filling those things, and filling those things, and they're always empty." I patiently explained that there was enough water in one bottle to supply one animal for about one hour, during the summer.

The best time for us was the evening, after the park was closed. Joy and I developed a nightly routine of uncapping a beer and strolling around the grounds. It was wonderful having the whole place to ourselves. The dogs gamboled about us, rushing off to explore this corner and that. Sinbad fell in love with the harbor seal (or, as the gift-shop manager referred to her, with his wonderful Down East accent, the "habbah seal"), and whenever we missed him we knew exactly where to start looking. Every night there was a battle to drag him away from the seal's pool and he sulked all the way back to the *Enterprise*, with his tail tucked between his legs.

These visits to the cages gradually eroded some of the hostility. I always carried along a bag of puffy cheese snacks, one of my many junk-food weaknesses, and the animals would hear the rattle of cellophane and go happily crazy in their cages. Even the baboon mellowed after a few evenings, hooting and leaping about with anticipation. At first he ripped the cheese puffs out of my hand and I had to be careful that he didn't take a finger or two as well, but with lots of patience and a soft voice I taught him to be gentle.

One night the teenager who helped out around the place forgot to lock the baboon's door. I was awakened in the morning by a banging racket and looked out the window to see the monkey experimentally opening and closing the door, apparently not sure what it all meant. I quickly called the dogs back into the trailer—the baboon, had he got loose, would have torn apart anything or anyone in his path—and then very carefully crept up on the cage and locked the door.

It was on one of our twilight strolls that we came upon a fenced-in area containing a few pigs. No water, no mud. The next morning I raised hell, again.

It didn't take us long to figure out why the waterfowl were screaming all the time. About a dozen ducks and geese drifted about on a shallow pond at the far end of the park. During the day, the fence enclosing the pond was opened so that the birds could wander among the visitors, cadging food. We observed very quickly that every time we ran water to cool the sun-baked stage or to hose down the cages, these birds would make a beeline for the puddles we left behind. When Joy noticed a drop in the water level of the pond, she realized she was watching the tide going out, and came shouting to me, "Ron! Ron! That's salt water, for crying out loud!" That afternoon, at our vehement insistence, plastic bowls and metal buckets were strung around the perimeter of the pond, and from then on Joy kept them filled with fresh water.

It wasn't all bad. The stage, when constructed, was adequate, although we had to use the *Enterprise* as a backdrop, creating problems with Hercules. At a very early age, he developed a phobia about the color white. And the *Enterprise* is a very large white thing. At Aqualand he refused to enter the stage via the ramp that passed by the rig and insisted upon approaching through the grass at the opposite end. But one afternoon, following a brief shower, he stepped out of his cage into a puddle. He likes water all right, when he's hot, but in the cool of a rain-washed afternoon he reacted the way any cat will, scrabbling backwards and shaking his paws in disgust. I was struggling to force him across the grass when he suddenly turned and galloped up the ramp, right past the *Enterprise*. From that day, the color of the fifth wheel ceased to be a problem.

And the audiences were marvelous. Our three-shows-a-day really packed the park, drawing people from all over the state. They were on the whole a rowdy lot, mostly working folk with small children by the hand. I soon realized that my black tights were out of place in this environment and, rather than endure laughter, or worse, I switched to a safari shirt and matching shorts.

Our animals were fascinated by their surroundings. From up on the stage they had unobstructed views in all directions of a variety of creatures they had never seen before. They evinced more curiosity than nervousness, so that during performances their heads were in constant motion. Hercules, for example, never took his eyes off Dandy, who came to the corner of her cage for each show and watched us intently. The audience often felt compelled to swivel around and see what our cats were staring at, a practice that caused mass embarrassment one day when Herk became intrigued by the sight of two goats doing what goats do best.

Despite our constant complaints and protests about Aqualand, the staff there became quite fond of us, even throwing a big party at the end of our stay.

Our two months at Aqualand came to an end at Labor Day. It was time to back the *Enterprise* out of the park, and Joy was a bundle of nerves anticipating a very difficult maneuver. The stage and bleachers were now additional factors, occupying as they did a great deal of the pull-forward room that had been vacant when we arrived. On the morning of our departure we were standing around the rig, chewing our nails and fretting through various schemes for backing up without demolishing anything. The main gate left only six inches to spare. Joy shook her head. "We're going to have to leave this one to God," she said, dismally.

A car pulled up, with a family of three who wanted to know what time the show would go on. They looked so disappointed when we said that our last show had been the day before that Joy offered to show them the animals, explaining that we had lots of time because we couldn't figure out how to back our trailer out of the park. "Can I help?" the man offered. "I'm a truck driver."

With Joy at the wheel and that wonderful man at the stern, the *Enterprise* was slowly, very slowly, inched through the gate. It got stuck in the mud once, and there wasn't enough room to pull forward for proper positioning, but after nearly three hours, we were free. The truck driver's wife and child stood by patiently through the ordeal, never uttering a word of complaint. When it was over, and everyone had breathed an audible sigh of relief, we asked how we could return the favor. All they wanted was a photograph of us, which they timidly requested we autograph.

15

After a few days with our families, we returned to St. Petersburg and promptly received a telegram inquiring about our availability for a new, one-ring circus being assembled by Serge Sachwyn. Sachwyn is the impresario who succeeded in bringing the Great Circus of China to Western audiences—a feat once considered impossible. In the last days of 1982 he was putting together the *"Festival Internationale du Cirque de Montréal,"* touted as featuring the best acts from around the world. Awards were to be presented under the aegis of the "Louis Cyr Competition." Louis Cyr was a turn-of-the-century strongman, a Quebeçois policeman who stood less than 6 feet tall, famous for his defeat of an 8-foot giant named Beaupré. He is a legend in Montreal.

While we promote ourselves as primarily a nightclub act, circuses have been a frequent and welcome factor in our lives. The mud show in Texas, Tihany's Mexican extravaganza and the abortive episode in Peru were just some of the many, many circuses we have appeared in. In the 1960s, when the big American circus was making a

190

comeback after years and years of decline, we had a visit from the producer of one of the biggest in the world. He expressed interest in us for an ice show, which didn't surprise us because these productions often feature "dry" acts. We agreed to give him a performance in our backyard, reasoning correctly that he had the imagination to envision how we looked with proper lighting.

The weather cooperated, and so did the animals, and we could see the producer was impressed. After the cats were returned to their cages, I suggested we adjourn to the house and talk a bit. The discussion was proceeding beautifully when suddenly the producer threw a totally unexpected curveball at us: "You will, of course, be performing on ice skates."

We gaped at him in stunned disbelief. Visions of trying to catch Venus while balancing on steel blades flashed through my head, followed by a rapid montage of Hercules balking at the cold under his feet, me falling on my rear end while carrying Joy over my head, and Joy, with her weak ankles, transformed from Pavlova to Chaplin. It was such a ridiculous idea we were speechless.

Finally I found my voice and protested that ice skates were out of the question for an act like ours. The producer became very indignant. The agent, who was standing out of his line of vision, began making frantic signals in an effort to shut me up, but I ignored him. There are some things that are not worth the money, and making fools of ourselves and our animals is at the top of that list.

The producer stormed out of the house and into his car, firing a parting shot to the effect that he didn't want an animal act for the ice show, anyway. We were much amused to see that one of his new shows featured Siegfried and Roy—and their animals.

The Montreal circus seemed definitely worth pursuing. We went through a few days of haggling about money, succeeding finally in getting what we wanted by convincing the producer to pay us in American, rather than Canadian dollars. The contract called for round-trip travel reimbursement and for a month's work plus one week's rehearsal time. The show was to be widely promoted, which indeed it was, although I doubt Serge Sachwyn anticipated the sort of publicity he ended up receiving.

In mid-December we were on our way again, back up through the latitudes and the increasing cold. We should have stopped off in Maine and left Pepe Taco with Joy's family but we were feeling adventurous and decided to smuggle him across the border. Not only does the parrot have no papers; it is illegal to transport such birds between countries because so many of them carry diseases. We crossed at Champlain, in New York, where experience has taught us we always get the least hassle. When the inspector approached, Pepe was in his little cage tucked under the dashboard of the pickup truck, heavily swathed in blankets to discourage his active tongue. The three of us were at the far end of the fifth wheel when Joy's acute hearing picked up the sound of a sopranic cadenza, muffled but audible. Before the inspector could cock an ear, she turned to me and said, "Ron, I think you left the radio on."

Oblivious, I replied blankly, "No, I didn't."

Joy looked me hard in the eye and hissed, very slowly, "Yes, you did, Ron. You left the *radio* on!"

Suddenly I understood and dashed back to the truck. Flinging open the door, I seized the cage and shook it violently, croaking, "SHUT UP!" Pepe lapsed into petulant silence.

As we pulled away from the border, Joy said emphatically, "Never again! We still have to get back with him!"

It was cold in Montreal. Not bitter, but cold enough. We were greatly relieved to find that the circus was being held in the comfortable and spacious Maurice Richard hockey arena. With the pets unloaded into the warm interior and the *Enterprise* pulled right up to a nearby door, we had an ideal arrangement for sleeping and never had to be more than a few steps away from them.

We were very surprised on arrival to receive instantaneous reimbursement for our one-way travel expenses.

The customary procedure is for the paying agent to review the receipts, double the amount, and dole out the full, round-trip cost when the show closes. The reasons for this quick payment eventually became clear.

Just before the grand opening on December 26th, two preview shows were held for disadvantaged children. They were more like dress rehearsals, giving us the chance to see how things went in real life without risking the wrath of a paying audience should events take an unfortunate turn. The producer was nervous. He came to our dressingroom for reassurance. "You know," he said, "this sort of leash act has never been done before in Canada. I mean, all those people so close to your animals. What would happen if one of them took off?" We explained to Serge that we hang onto the leash no matter what, that a frightened cat will almost always head immediately for his cage, and that we are in control at all times. He shook his head and looked apprehensive, but there was nothing else we could tell him.

Almost prophetically, when the time came for Hercules to leave his cage and come to the center of the ring, he balked. Despite our constant reminders to the butchers to stay away when we're performing, a balloon vendor walked into Herk's line of vision. The tiger backed stubbornly into the safety of his cage and parked his haunches down as if to say, "I am not moving." To the audience's delight, I talked him out, sitting down beside him and saying things like, "Hercules, do you want to do the finale now? Come on, Herk, come with Dad." When he finally summoned his courage and stepped onto the floor, there was thunderous applause. Serge was back in our dressingroom after the show. "Ron and Joy," he said, "you were right. I'm not going to worry any more."

The audiences were fantastic. Oh, how good it felt to be received with such overwhelming and delighted enthusiasm! Joy, with her fluent and correct French, became the talk of the town, appearing on dozens of interview shows, including a two-hour radio program of the call-and-ask-questions type. The subway walls were lined with gigantic posters announcing the circus, all of them featuring Joy and Hercules on the mirror ball. We couldn't have prepared a better set-up if we had done it ourselves.

We took two of the four Louis Cyr awards, which were presented weekly during the run of the show. The prizes were large, wooden plaques mounted with a color photograph of Louis Cyr, and engraved with our names and awards: Best Showmanship and Most Popular Act.

Nothing is perfect in this world. At the beginning of the third week of the circus' month-long engagement, Serge called all the performers together and announced that the box office was not doing well. There were a couple of reasons, none of them as obvious to Serge as they were to us. By opening the circus right after Christmas, he had lost a great many people who were out of funds following that expensive holiday, people whose budgets were unlikely to recover in only a week or two. And he was touting the show more as a European-style evening of entertainment than as a circus, in an effort to pull in the class of people who could afford the higher-than-usual ticket price.

"There's a chance," he told us, "that we'll close down after this week." Several people asked when he would know for certain, but he would say only, "This decision will go right down to the wire." We all agreed to wait it out, but we made it clear that we expected notice of some sort.

A member of the lighting crew ventured the opinion that the show was not being properly advertised, that the promotional effort was lacking. Since I found it hard to argue with seven-foot posters of my wife all over the subway system, I stood up and disagreed with him, saying that I thought promotion was not the problem.

From the moment I opened my mouth at that meeting, Joy and I became involuntarily associated with the producer. The rest of the troupe immediately perceived us as being on "his side," as allies, even as apple-polishers. We turned a lot of them around in the week that followed, but when things began to fall apart, there were still a few who watched us with jaundiced eyes. The producer, in turn, did nothing to dispel this image, calling the other performers' attention to us frequently as examples of expertise to be emulated. We were in an awkward position. As the week came to an end, everyone was asking everyone else if anyone had heard anything. "Are we closing? Are we closing?" When no announcements were forthcoming, the troupe prepared for its usual two shows on Sunday, the beginning of the fourth week. After the first show I noticed one of the lighting men taking down a piece of equipment and asked him what he was doing. "Oh, I want to be ready to ship all this stuff out tomorrow."

"What?" I asked.

"Never mind, never mind, forget it," he said, hastily.

It was inconceivable that the show would close without warning, so I said nothing and we did the second show. No sooner were we back in our dressingroom than the conductor appeared, carrying our music in his hand. "Back to you," he said, handing the papers to Joy.

"What's this?" she asked.

"Didn't you know? The show's closed." Then he saw our astonishment and added, "Oh, I'm sorry. I thought you knew." And hurried away.

Word of the unannounced closing spread rapidly through the arena, and Serge had so many angry performers on his hands that he hastily called a meeting, for which he supplied free beer in an obvious attempt to soothe the ragged edges. He was very subdued, so subdued in fact that people in the back row of the angry circle kept yelling, "We can't hear you!" and "Speak up!"

Through the mumbling came the essence of Serge's message. The show was closed. Pressed for an explanation for his lack of notice, he mentioned a couple of people who had known, as though somehow telling a prop man or some other worker should have been sufficient for all. Before the producer could melt away, one of the women in the trapeze act asked about the extra day's pay. The show week ran from Sunday to Saturday; we had worked that very day, a Sunday, so we were due another day's salary. The implication was obvious: Serge didn't tell us about the closing for fear we would refuse to work past the third week. His response to the trapeze artist, "I don't wish to discuss it," sent the entire group into a rage.

Someone now inquired about the return transportation costs, to which Serge replied that we should all send him our receipts when we got home and he would reimburse us by mail. This suggestion was met by hoots of derision. Credibility was lost.

Looking back on his behavior, it seems self-evident that if he had been straightforward and honest, if he had simply told the troupe that he didn't have the money but would send salaries as funds came in, most of us would have been willing to meet him halfway. What he was doing was "stonewalling."

I got to my feet. "Listen, Mr. Sachwyn," I said, very slowly, "when I get screwed, I like to *enjoy* it!" And I turned on my heel and headed for the door. This was all the proof any hold-outs needed to be convinced that I wasn't an agent of the producer.

A burly Swiss from the sway-pole act, a lovable bear of a man well known to be always one beat behind, now stormed up to Serge and screamed at him, "You mean you're not going to pay us?"

Serge lifted a disdainful eyebrow. "How dare you talk to me like that!" he sneered. "Why don't you go back to your mudshow!"

The Swiss grabbed him by the collar and lifted him off the floor. "You know what they do in mudshows? When the man has no money, he hocks his watch, or anything he can, to pay his people. That's what they do in mudshows!"

Serge was still dangling in the air but he wasn't intimidated. "And if they don't?"

"If they don't," bellowed the Swiss, "they get broken in half!" With that he drew back a fist to leave his mark on Serge's nose, but the sway-poler's brother quickly intervened and convinced him to put the producer back on his feet.

With a lot of grumbling and some tears, the group slowly disbanded, many of them ending up with us in our dressingroom. Already, through no direct action on our part, we were being set off as the leaders, the people to turn to during crisis. We were sitting around discussing our options when Serge and his assistant, Peter, suddenly popped in. "Ron," gushed Serge, as though nothing had happened, "the video tapes came in and they look great! Come see them!" I recognized this as another attempt to isolate us from the pack, but I wanted to go to the viewing, too. Reluctantly, I tagged along after the two of them. Serge pulled up a seat next to mine and blithely helped himself to my popcorn. He seemed to have no sense of the fitness of things.

We're a little vague as to how the sit-in actually got started. Joy remembers approaching one of the Swiss brothers to apologize for my language during the meeting and making the statement, "We're not leaving until we get our money." Within a matter of minutes some sort of understanding among the performers resulted in a blockade of the building's entrances. Trucks and trailers were driven into the doorways, effectively sealing the place off to all motorized traffic.

Since the last show had started at five o'clock, the evening was relatively young, leaving Joy ample time to take advantage of all the media contacts she had made during her interviews. Soon the place was crawling with reporters and cameramen, some of them wringing human interest material out of the couples with young children. Joy became the spokesperson, partly because of her language facility, partly because we had always been perceived by the other acts as "different," set apart somehow by our reputations, our nightclub background, our willingness to speak up and to grab the bull by the horns.

A sort of armed camp developed. Serge, finding himself cast in the role of villain, told the press that Joy was a troublemaker and then took off, leaving Peter holding the

197

bag. It was Peter who was forced to deal with the blockade and related problems, like the ongoing advertising. Serge neglected to cancel television commercials touting the show, and during the sit-in we encountered weary travelers, sometimes from a whole province away, puzzled and angry outside the gate because the ads had said nothing about a closing date. The newspapers threw the issue of the ads into the campaign, adding fuel to the fire.

A few of the performers had other bookings and left, but the majority, having nowhere to go for the week they had expected to work in Montreal, settled in for a siege. Arena management was wonderful. They, too, had no plans for the week, and they went about making us as comfortable as possible and even brought in food. In turn, some of the acts, notably a generous and kind-hearted Polish couple, insisted on feeding the few arena employees who were forced to stick around supplying heat and light.

Our self-imposed confinement lasted four days, during which the newspapers had a field day, with regular, front-page photostories about our difficulties. But we were all showing signs of wear and tear. When Peter appeared on the fourth day to deliver the engraved tags for our two awards, Joy saw an opportunity to break the blockade. As she accepted the plaques, she started to walk away and then turned back. "Peter!" she pleaded. "Won't you at least talk to these people? We're not idiots. We know there isn't any money. But if you offered to try, if you even gave out letters promising to try to do something later, this would all be over."

Peter looked doubtful. "Oh, yeah," he said, "but they don't understand. . . . "

Joy interrupted. "Peter, *we're* 'they.' *I* am 'they.' All this time you've been trying to set us apart from the others, but we are a part of them, we're all performers. At least come talk to us."

Peter said he would try. Joy found most of the performers gathered in the arena office and asked them how they felt about a letter over Peter's signature. At this point we were all willing to take whatever we could get.

Peter disappeared and returned later in the day with letters for everybody. We almost missed getting one because, as he made his rounds of the arena, he saw the press calling on us again, and trotting past our trailer he bellowed, "You're not getting a letter until you get rid of them!" We agreed to do as he asked but instead we allowed the reporter, cameraman and lightman to sneak into our trailer, and Joy got in one last interview before the siege broke and the performers began to disband. In the end we got our letter, for all it was worth.

We never saw a cent of the money promised in it and to the best of our knowledge neither did anyone else.

16

We crossed the border at Champlain again, on our way back to Maine for a three-week layover. The immigration and customs people had been following our plight in the newspapers and they all wanted to know how we'd come through.

Our next booking, the Garden Circus, opened in Cornwall, Ontario, and then moved on to various Canadian cities. Ian Garden's production is the Canadian equivalent of the U.S.'s Ringling Circus, a three-ring affair, on a smaller scale. Its primary source of income is Shrine dates. Garden himself is a wonderful man, a sort of Canadian version of Tihany—honest, straightforward, generous—a pleasure to work for.

This was the circus mentioned earlier, where our cats had their first exposure to other, large animals, in close quarters. By the time Garden's circus reached its third city, Toronto, the really awful smells from the arena-act cats were beginning to get to us. Here all the cages—the arena cats, ours, and everyone else's—were crammed backstage, bumper to bumper, as it were, and the ammonia fumes from the neglected tigers and lions were so bad that even our eyes were watering. Joy started on the trainer almost at once, chiding him good-naturedly about his neglect. Over the course of our four days in that city she gradually shamed him into taking proper care of his cats, at least while he was around us.

Word of an impending visit from the humane society caused us no concern. It should have worried the arena man, but either he didn't care or he didn't find out in time. The trainer of the chimps, on the other hand, got so rattled he forgot to lock one of his cages, and a large female primate escaped and then freed two compatriots. The three of them got out of the truck, which was parked by the stage door, and onto the sidewalk, dangerously close to the traffic, creating chaos for about two hours until they were captured by their trainer with assistance from the police.

Trailing a couple of newspapermen who were undoubtedly looking for a story about shameful conditions behind the scenes, the humane society representative made his way into the crowded corner where our cages and those of the arena cats were jammed into a smelly menage. I was tired and also irritated from being trapped around the clock with the noisome tigers and the complaining lions, so I was in no mood to be conciliatory. When one of the group approached Magic's cage, wrinkled his nose and asked, "Do you think he's happy in there?" my hackles went straight up.

"I don't know," I said with mock concern, "why don't we ask him?" I sidled over to the cage and bent down to Magic's serene face, my voice dripping with sarcasm. "Are we unhappy? Do we want to come out?" Then I flung open the door and stepped away.

The group froze. Magic snarled and hissed a bit, but he didn't move. Slowly the reporters backed away, until they were flat against the opposite wall, and then one of them stuttered, "If you're doing that for our benefit, you've made your point. Please close that door!"

One of the newspaper photographers had eyes sharp enough to notice that while the smells were everywhere, our cages were too clean to be part of the problem. He snapped a fabulous picture of Magic framed by the cage door, paws crossed languidly in front of him, enormous green eyes staring straight ahead. Returning later in the tour, he apologized for the assumptions of his coworkers and presented us with a color print of the leopard that we cherish.

We had marvelous success in Toronto. All the wrinkles had been ironed out, everyone's animals performed beautifully, and the audiences were wonderful. We had a large, quality orchestra here, and proper spotlights. The first time those lights hit the mirror ball with Herk and Joy atop, and the reflections spun madly around the arena, the kids screamed with such delight that for a second Joy thought some animal had got loose and began looking wildly around for an impending disaster.

The Garden show moved on to Montreal, but we had a restrictive clause in our contract with the *Festival Internationale* prohibiting us from performing there for thirty days after that circus closed. We decided to move on and await Garden's show in the next city, Allentown, Pennsylvania, taking our time as we went.

Thus began what we call The Border Wars.

When we cross into Canada we have to make three stops: the vet, customs, and immigration. Each crossing is different, depending on the size of the station, how busy it is when we come through, the moods of the individual inspectors. We are hauling an enormous and heavy trailer, we have animals that need to be fed and cleaned and exercised regularly, and we are driving a truck that, on a good stretch, might pump out five miles to the gallon. In short, we try to plan each trip for maximum efficiency.

We have papers upon papers upon papers. In 1974 a lot of new laws governing the ownership, sale, and transport of endangered species hit the books, and these statutes have been amended, modified, altered, deleted and reinstated a million times since then. It's all Joy can do to keep up with the regulations. At one time, for example, a person wishing to own a tiger had to prove that the animal was born in captivity. Then the law was rewritten requiring proof that the animal was *conceived* in captivity. A tiger owner in Sarasota, in possession of papers showing her breeding female was born here, could scarcely be expected to drag the animal to India for implanting by a wild tiger. It would seem sufficient for the owner to prove that the parents are natives, assuming of course one could identify the parents. An owner with six males and four females would rarely know whom to credit for offspring. . . .

Normally at the Canadian border the officials get very busy with our sheafs of U.S. permits. We have health certificates for the dogs, too, but once the inspectors see what we're hauling they lose all interest in the canines. Should we ever have the need, we could probably cross with two hydrophobic dogs, complete with foam mustaches.

The most direct route to Allentown was via the Thousand Islands Crossing. Here we ran into our first barrier. The inspector asked what we were hauling, and Joy told him.

"Oh?" was the response.

Ever cheerful, Joy let out a hearty guffaw. "Ah," she said, "you don't believe me."

"That's not it," he replied, looking worried. "I think you've just driven 200 miles out of your way."

An endless telephone conversation followed, with some man in a central position of authority, somewhere. Our inspector seemed to be trying to find out whether it was legal for us to cross at Thousand Islands and whether or not we needed some sort of manifest that we apparently should have picked up on our way into Canada. Nobody, of course, had said a word about these forms when we left the States.

Joy finally got on the line to untangle the mess and found herself talking to a very rude individual who gave her a lecture: "Ignorance of the law is no excuse. If you read your federal papers," he growled, "you'd know the only places you can cross in New York are Buffalo, Champlain or Lewiston."

Joy had indeed read those papers, but the language was confusing, and she had interpreted them to say that these were only some of the places available to us.

Joy then asked if we could cross at Champlain without the manifest, but the answer was, "If they let you through, they'll be breaking the law." The parting shot was "Just be grateful I don't hit you with a five-hundred-dollar fine, lady." Joy thanked him profusely and only the inspectors at our end could see the sarcasm on her face.

It was 11 o'clock in the morning and we were determined not to arrive at any crossing, wherever it was, at five in the afternoon, when the key people at these stations usually go off duty. We took off at top speed, sliding through Montreal at four o'clock, which wasn't easy, heading for Champlain, a known quantity and closer than Buffalo. It was nearly five when we pulled up to the station. The guards took one look at our papers and said, "Oh, you're the people they called us about." (Son of a bitch, I thought, he wasn't happy fouling us up at Thousand Islands.) But the next words were, "Those lousy feds, they have nothing to do but make trouble. This piece of paper, that piece of paper, and you know what? You'll come back here next month and you won't need either of them—it'll be *another* piece of paper! They're insane with their forms."

The guard took our papers inside, looked them over, and came out again. "What day did you go into Canada?"

Joy checked her papers. "February seventeenth."

"Good enough." The guard filled in the missing form, gave us a few extra blanks for the next time, and waved us through, adding, "Don't be surprised if no one ever asks for that form again."

He was almost right. After Allentown and Reading we returned to Kitchener, Ontario, crossing as warned at Buffalo. But we were also told *not* to come back through Buffalo because the U.S. side no longer had a vet on duty. Joy was very skeptical and kept saying, "Are you sure?" They were sure: Lewiston was now the place for reentry.

When our three-city tour in Ontario was over and we came to the Lewiston crossing, we were raked over the coals as though we were trying to smuggle Iranian gunrunners, until Joy produced the manifests. Another couple, right behind us with a trailer full of lions, also produced the unexpected forms, the extras given to us in Champlain. The officials were surprised as hell to see those papers—the four of us probably spoiled a lot of fun for them.

Crossing into Canada is never nearly as bad as trying to break back into our own country. Apparently a bureaucracy is a bureaucracy is a bureaucracy. Ironically, as so often is the case, the real trouble is often overlooked while the inspectors go digging around for an excuse to cause mischief. We're always asked if we're carrying firearms. We always say "no." Gun powder? Hell, yes, we've got tons of that, but nobody ever asks! We use it and other explosive material to create the fire and flashpot in the magic mirror ball. We've gone back and forth across the border dozens of times with that stuff, but it's always the same: Papers. They want to see The Papers.

* * *

Sometimes life, having unmercifully rained blows on our heads for what seems like months on end, hands us something truly special that seems to make it all worthwhile. Two years after our letdown in Las Vegas and a year after the sit-in in Canada, we signed a contract to appear as the special guest stars of a European-style revue that was to run the entire summer of 1984 at, of all places, Radio City Music Hall. It was an emotional high, going home to that hallowed building after so many years. Even the star was an old friend—Liliane Montevecchi, with whom we had worked some sixteen years before in *Les Girls! Les Girls!* The show, *Gotta Getaway*, was a hit, the subways were adorned with bigger-than-life posters of Joy riding the mirror ball with Hercules, our quarters were comfortable and homey, New York City was its old exciting self, and we had the time of our lives. Sometimes, it all comes together.

PART
4

People
and Places

1

There's an old saying in show biz that the "bigger" a star is, the easier he or she is to get along with. Our experience with "headliners" over the past 25 years has certainly proved this to be true. We have supported some of the biggest names in the business and can truly say that with one or two minor (very minor) exceptions, they have invariably gone out of their way to be kind, courteous, appreciative and just plain nice to us.

Years of observation have convinced us that in most cases the real stars are beyond the point of feeling threatened by the likes of us, and are sure enough of themselves that they don't need to get their jollies by making the little folk feel bad. It's purely a question of self-confidence and self-assurance, as in any other walk of life. Oh, there is the exception, the person whose head has become so swollen with self-importance that he doesn't stoop to speaking with his inferiors. We have been lucky enough to run across very few of these.

Agents, on the other hand, are another story. Their dog-eat-dog, gotta-make-a-buck environment often breeds indifference bordering on cruelty. And, of course, occasionally just plain dishonesty.

It was very early in our adagio career when we came upon an agent who was a cliché out of a Grade-B Hollywood drama. At the time we were poorer than church mice, still living in our rathole on Carmine Street with a portfolio that was virtually a blank sheet. Somehow we made contact with an agent who was responsible for booking practically every act that appeared on the *Ed Sullivan Show*, then at the peak of its popularity. More than one nobody had become a somebody overnight because of a single appearance on that show. Getting a booking there meant the world to us.

When the Big Man, as we dubbed the agent, agreed to give us an audition, we dug deep into our pockets and found enough money to rent a small studio near his CBS office. It would have been nice of him to have loaned us a room at CBS, but "nice" wasn't in his vocabulary.

The audition went well. The Big Man seemed impressed. We were told to come to his office the following afternoon. All agog with excitement and almost overcome with anticipation, we were shown from his plush lobby into the throne room, where the agent sat at an enormous desk, intimidatingly raised off the floor like a judge's bench. All around us were leather chairs and thick carpeting, and off to one side stood a couch that appeared to be covered in zebra skin. The Big Man went into his Hollywood spiel, talking fast and chewing on a mangled cigar. It was almost impossible to understand him but eventually the message came through. "Listen," he said, rocketing the cigar around between his teeth, "you kids, you're gonna get three grand for the shot on Sullivan and this is what you're gonna do. When you get that check for three grand, you sign the whole thing over to me and I'll see that you really make it big in this city."

We were so naive we thought we could bargain. "Gee," ventured Joy, "we really need that money for costumes and arrangements. We're so broke we're working in leotards to a record. Couldn't we borrow some of it?" The

209

head shook, the cigar waggled back and forth. "We'll be nice to you," she went on, not realizing the hole she was digging, "we'll pay you back every cent."

"You want to be nice to me?" the agent asked. "You!" he jabbed a finger in my direction. "You go down to the coffee shop and leave me alone with your wife for an hour." The jabbing finger poked a button on the desk and darned if that zebra couch didn't flip out into a bed. We gaped at it.

"But," babbled Joy, and how ridiculous we must have sounded, "we're married."

"Good," grunted the Big Man, "if you get knocked up, he can take the rap for me!"

Our protests went unheard, eventually shouts were exchanged, and we found ourselves back on the street. For years afterward, agents, managers and producers who tried to get us booked on the Sullivan show could never understand the brick wall they banged into. The Big Man was as powerful as he was immoral, and he made up his mind that Ron and Joy Holiday would never work that show. Even Russell Markert at Radio City Music Hall failed, as did the producer at the Latin Quarter.

We cried when we left that man's office and, though we put him behind us and went on with our pursuits, we have never forgotten him. We are not ashamed to admit that over the years we have wished him ill, many times, especially because it seemed that everyone in the world either claimed to have seen us on the Sullivan show, or offered to place us there, or asked us why we never did it. After a comedian in the Borscht Belt introduced us as "direct from the Ed Sullivan Show," I pulled him aside, set him straight, and then began writing our own introductions, to make sure that never happened again.

We were still rather naive and trusting a couple of years later when we agreed to dance at a *haute couture* fashion show. Sharing the spotlight with us were some very funny comedians, including Jackie Mason. The booking agent was a nervous wreck, treating us all as if we had never worked professionally before, but somehow we managed to perform in spite of him. The performers were to be paid their rather generous salaries at the end of the show, but while Jackie Mason was on stage breaking up the audience, the booking agent suffered a heart attack and was taken to the hospital. When the show was over, we were all wandering around asking who was going to pay us, at which point the show's manager volunteered to lay out the money himself until he could be reimbursed. It wasn't until we were about to leave the hotel that I opened our pay envelope, and found considerably more money than we had contracted for. Curious, I went back to the manager and asked if perhaps he had made a mistake in our salary. He looked thoughtful for a moment and then said, "Oh, yes, I forgot to deduct the agent's ten percent. Would you mind giving it to him directly?"

But the ten percent didn't account for the difference. The booking agent, in a time-honored tradition, had quoted the fashion show organizers a price for, say, Jackie Mason, quoted Mason's agent a lower salary, and planned to pocket the difference. There is no doubt that this double bookkeeping trick had been pulled on us many, many times, but this was the first time the agent was caught *in flagrante delicto*, and, more important, this time we could do something about it.

In the morning, as soon as the bank opened, I cashed the check and then deposited the cash into our savings account. Simultaneously, Joy sent the booking agent a check for ten percent of the salary he had quoted us. Less than three days later our phone rang right off the wall, and there was the booking agent, obviously risking a relapse, threatening to sue, promising us we would never work again, and so on. Finally I told him, "Don't be yelling at me. There are good crooks and stupid crooks, and you were a stupid crook—you got caught. It was up to you to have your heart attack *after* you'd paid us." And I hung up.

The entertainment business, like any other, is a learning process for anyone venturing into it. Perhaps there are more sharks, more pitfalls, more potential problems because of the big money always lying about and because of the monster egos (mine included) that must meet, work together and part as civilly as possible. Most of the lessons are nonverbal, for anyone willing to watch and learn.

A sense of person and of place, as in all aspects of life, seems to bring equanimity and security. We saw this so clearly one night when we shared the bill with Alan King at a club date in Detroit. As the act that opened the show, we could leave early in the evening, our work done, and, as was our custom, grab a plane back to Newark and be home in time for the *Late Show*. But King was on a tight schedule that required him to dash straight to the airport after his performance, so he asked us if, instead of rushing off, we would hold a cab for him. As he finished his bows, he literally ran out of the club into the taxi we had standing by, and at the airport he insisted on paying for the ride. Since the plane was delayed, he suggested hot dogs all around.

Our waitress recognized King at once and was very excited to be serving a celebrity. She took our order and then rushed back to share her thrill with a coworker. The coworker seemed determined to avoid appearing impressed, because she brayed in clarion tones that bounced off the four walls, "Alan King? Who the *hell* is Alan King?" We nearly died of embarrassment until we turned to look at King. There was no indication on his face or in his manner that he had heard one word of that outburst. He went right on talking to us as though nothing had happened. When you know who you are. . . .

And when you know who you are, you not only don't mind lack of recognition, you don't mind being overlooked completely. When we worked at the Concord in the Catskills we were in the habit of eating early so that our food would be well settled before we began dancing. A call to room service produced a formal waiter with linen-covered table and all the trimmings, and we dined in style. Rather than shove the table out into the hall, I always called for a busboy to pick it up, but one night I had no sooner cradled the telephone receiver when I heard noises at the door. "Boy, that busboy came fast," I said to Joy, as I opened the door. I had just showered and was traipsing about the room with only a towel around my waist. I indicated the dinner table to the thin little black man who stood in the doorway and turned to resume my toilette. "Yassa, yassa, Ah's comin, Ah gots it, yassa." I couldn't believe my ears. Whirling around, I was horrified to see that I had mistaken Sammy Davis, Jr., for the busboy.

Completely unperturbed, Davis trucked over to the table, doing a buck-and-wing as he went, turned it around and wheeled it toward the door. "Oh, my God! I'm sorry!" I wailed. Davis laughed. Our rooms were right next to each other, and what I had heard was his struggle to make his key fit in our door. Quite the opposite of being offended, he thought the whole thing was so funny that he told the orchestra about it, and when we appeared for our performance we were ribbed unmercifully.

A breathtaking demonstration of coolness under pressure came from a relatively unknown performer, one we will never forget. Wayne Newton was to headline at Blinstrub's in Boston one week shortly after his initial success, "Red Roses for a Blue Lady." He arrived with his brother, who accompanied him on the guitar. The two of them were as easygoing and humble as they could be. Memories of how close they had come to throwing in the towel were still alive. Newton told us that they had spent their last dime to make the "Red Roses" recording, and had vowed that if it failed they were quitting the business. They seemed to be on their way now, but everyone in show business knows that the key word is "fickle."

Newton's brother went to see the orchestra leader, Mr. Gaylord, to make arrangements for rehearsals. Gaylord was a tough cookie. He bowed to no one and he was famous for his biting personality. Open and friendly, Newton's brother held out his hand and gushed, "Hi! I'm Wayne Newton's brother." Gaylord raised one eyebrow, looked down his nose and said, coldly, "Who?"

Undaunted, the Newton brothers got through their rehearsals and were doing well on opening night until the late show, which, as so often happens, produced a noisy crowd that was too drunk to appreciate the artist. One of Newton's numbers was a beautifully staged piece in which he sat at a dressing table on an otherwise dark stage applying clown makeup while singing "Be a Clown." He followed this with a monologue in which he wandered aimlessly around the stage, wiping off the clown face and asking imaginary friends if they wanted to join him for the evening, but each of these invisible people was too busy to spend time with him. Then he walked to the front of the stage, with just a pinspot on his face and, looking very sad, began to softly sing "Who Can I Turn To?" But the revelers in the audience were drowning him out.

From the door of our dressingroom we watched Newton very, very slowly lower the microphone away from his mouth until it was dangling from the end of his arm like a dead lizard. He kept right on singing, and Gaylord, who at this point must have been regretting his rudeness, kept right on conducting. Suddenly it got very quiet in the room. For a second there wasn't a sound. Then the audience began quieting itself. Elbows nudged ribs, bursts of "Shut up," and "Hush," and "Hey, the kid is singing" echoed around the club. Without missing a beat Newton slowly raised the mike back to his mouth, and this time the audience hung on his every note. He then got three standing ovations, an honor he received at each performance at Blinstrub's. He earned our admiration, and Gaylord's, and that of a lot of other people that night. His success today testifies to that early showmanship.

Pros are like that. It's more than "the show must go on." It means keeping on with the show even when everything goes wrong. It means helping other performers when they get into trouble, on stage or off. It means tolerance and understanding and cooperation and a hundred other things that no one who hasn't stood before an audience can ever understand. Stars have done things for us probably without thinking, just because that's the nature of the business.

At one appearance at the Belleview-Stratford in Philadelphia, a few years before it was blighted with the first known attack of Legionnaire's Disease, we supported Bob Hope. The star of the show always closes the evening, but on this occasion Hope had a conflict in schedule and was forced to open the show. This was unheard of. We were in a panic at the thought of following him, envisioning most if not all of the audience rising en masse after his act and dribbling out the door to the strains of our music. But he surprised us completely. Just before his closing jokes he suddenly said, "Before I go, I must tell you, I know two very talented dancers who are waiting in the wings. Please do me the honor, since I have to leave, of watching these kids. I know you're going to love them. Give them the same chance you would give me." And they did. We got a terrific reception. It was a marvelous thing for Hope to do and we have never forgotten it.

When you know for certain who you are, you have nothing to hide. I was taught a very valuable lesson in self-respect by none other than the grandest lady of them all, Marlene Dietrich. She was scheduled to follow us at the Concord and we couldn't resist hanging around an extra day to see her. There had been all manner of backbiting and snide remarks as her performance approached, most of it centered around whether she had or hadn't had a face lift or other cosmetic surgery. Shuffling around backstage, I happened upon her quite by chance as she lay back on one of those gadgets designed to hold a performer semi-upright so that the costume doesn't get wrinkled. She was wearing a skintight white gown and a fur coat that dripped fox upon fox upon fox, halfway to the next county. I couldn't take my eyes off her. I must have been gaping like a backwoods hick because she finally smiled at me and purred, "Did you want to ask me something?" I blubbered and babbled for a minute and then managed to say that I thought she was the most beautiful woman I'd ever seen, and then I ran off at the mouth for a bit

215

about what fantastic care she must take of herself, dieting all the time and what have you. She smiled at me again. "Darling," she said, holding a hand flat under her chin, "take care of yourself from here down, and science will take care of from here up." Like a star-struck teenager I dashed off to tell Joy I'd met Marlene Dietrich. "You see," I told her, "she *has* had a face lift. But so what? You could perform that same surgery on a fat old cow and you wouldn't end up with Marlene Dietrich." I suspect that no one was more aware of this than Marlene herself.

Totie Fields, whose premature departure from this world we have much mourned, gave us a demonstration one night of just how far a headliner will go to support the other members of the cast. We were telling her at a club date in the Borscht Belt how upset we were by the maître d's habit of holding the ringside tables for the big tippers. For an opening act, as we were that night, this practice can be very annoying, producing a noisy, shuffling distraction that is hard on the audience and on the performers. Hearing our complaints, Totie looked out from behind the curtain, saw the empty tables near the stage, and without a word to us went to a nearby backstage phone and demanded to speak to the maître d'. He must have tried to protest because she became infuriated, shrieking at him that nobody, absolutely nobody, was going to go on until every table at ringside was full. She began jumping up and down with rage, and actually broke the heels off both of her shoes. Then she turned calmly back to us and said, "That should take care of it." A few minutes later the maître d' telephoned back and asked if she was satisfied. She peeked out, looked around, and agreed to let the show start. We were amazed at her indignation on our behalf, and grateful for her concern.

It's funny now to look back on some of the struggling hopefuls we encountered here and there, and see what's become of them. One we remember very clearly from our early adagio days, when we were invited to appear on Rudy Vallee's TV show, *On Broadway Tonight*. Eartha Kitt was on the same show, as was a young black comedian whose career wasn't moving along very well at all. He often sat with us at the automat and told us how lucky we were to have played Radio City and to be working regularly. His name was Richard Pryor.

Before we became an animal act, we were almost invariably supporters of name stars and very, very rarely the main attraction. We were, therefore, seldom in a position to return the kindness that was so often shown to us. But very early in our adagio career the hand we held out to one lonely and introverted man resulted in an extraordinary and unforgettable friendship.

During our first lean winter as adagio performers and dance instructors at the Casa Marina in Key West, we were introduced to Tennessee Williams. Our mutual acquaintance felt that since we were both "in the theater," we would find each other interesting company. To our embarrassment, we didn't even know who he was, nor did we learn how famous he was until we heard the guests talking about him.

The Casa Marina was Tennessee's winter headquarters. He arrived each year with his elderly mother, who called him "Tom," and his secretary. He spent most of his time engrossed in his writing, but when he felt like getting out and moving around, he was helpless; his driver's license had expired and all his attempts to pass the test for its renewal ended in failure. His shocking-pink Thunderbird sat idle. Spurred by his need for a driver and armed with lessons from a master, my wife, I went with him on his fourth and final assault on the Department of Highway Safety and I passed the test with a perfect score. I remember Tennessee's dismay when he failed yet again, and the surprise on the trooper's face when I pointed out the tiny lady who had taught me so well. In any event, with both of us now licensed, Tennessee had a pair of able and willing chauffeurs, and we were more than delighted to take him wherever he wanted to go.

Often Tennessee joined us on our daily pilgrimage to the end of the dock, where we could sit surrounded by the warm sun and the pellucid sea. He would sit off to one

217

side, his work in his lap, and from time to time he would shout over to Joy for help with spelling, an area that appeared to give him tremendous difficulty. During that winter, he worked constantly on *Night of the Iguana.*

Tennessee was not a popular guest at the Casa Marina. The place dripped snobbery from every chandelier, and he was the object of not-very-subtle ridicule, even disgust. The words "dirty old man" and "trash" were on the lips of people who really had no idea what sort of person he was, but the rumors about his sexual preferences were reason enough to ostracize him. In truth, he was a very likable and generous fellow. It was all we could do to bite our collective lip in the evening when he would stroll out of the hotel, and some blue-blooded guest would look down his nose and say, "There he goes, off to cruise the naval base." Not once during that winter or the next, when we all met again at Key West, did we know him to do anything of the kind. On one or two weekends each season he would place a call to New York and a handsome young male "model" would arrive to share Tennessee's quarters. His demeanor and behavior scarcely justified the treatment he received from the other guests, or the verbal garbage they leveled at him behind his back. Joy was dancing with him one evening when a man came up to me and snarled, "If that were my wife, I certainly wouldn't let her dance with *him.* He's trash."

The playwright's tales of his work were fascinating to us. "People always ask me how my imagination can create all those places and characters. The truth is, they're all real. I meet the most incredible people as I travel around the country, staying in small hotels in dinky towns, hanging out in local bars. Nothing I could create from my head would begin to equal the weird and wonderful things I see and hear in those places."

We frequently went out to dinner with Tennessee. All of us would get tired now and then of hotel cuisine, even though for Joy and me it was a free ride. He often insisted on picking up the tab and wouldn't hear our protests. "Please let me do this," he urged us. "You're such great

218

company—and I call great company people who know when someone wants to be left alone." He seemed to mean that not only did we respect his privacy, we also did not judge. There were so many people around him eager to put him down, to condemn and insult, without ever giving him the chance to show what a truly warm and generous person he was.

2

In the fall of 1971 we saw the movie "Midnight Cowboy" and decided we didn't want to grow old in a cold, urban environment. "Everybody waits to move to Florida until they're past enjoying it," I told Joy. "Let's do it now." Friends and associates quickly assured us that moving away from the "action" was professional suicide, but we reasoned that contracts can be mailed and it seemed likely that even Florida had a telephone system.

I knew exactly what I wanted, having been influenced to Mediterranean Revival architecture by that pleasure dome of Key West, the Casa Marina. An uncle who had spent years in Florida buying and remodeling houses put us in touch with a real estate agent who eventually found the very house I had in mind, right down to the details, but I took one look at it and said, "Oh, no, there's no way we can afford that." Located one block from the water at the southern end of the St. Petersburg peninsula, where Tampa Bay meets the Gulf of Mexico, the immense beige-stucco house sat in a veritable wilderness of overgrown streets. The neighborhood contained perhaps two other homes and was still zoned agricultural.

The real estate agent cleverly showed us we could afford the house, as these people are wont to do, and between bookings we moved in.

The house was, and is, a St. Petersburg historical landmark, dating from 1926, when it was a summer residence for one of St. Petersburg's most eminent ladies, Mrs. Tippetts. Mrs. Tippetts was quite a character. She supervised every facet in the construction of her home, to the point of going out into the bay with the men hired to collect coral for the trim. She personally examined every piece, rejecting those that didn't meet her standards for shape and color. She must have been a royal pain in the neck.

When Mrs. Tippetts eventually went off to a nursing home, she left behind all her notes on the house, as well as diaries and letters. We found a box full of these papers in the attic, undisturbed by the intervening years and owners. They revealed her interest in the Audubon Society, in local civic affairs (the house was a polling place at one time because it was the only large building on the south side of the city), and in the immediate neighborhood. Mrs. Tippetts was virtually the only occupant of what is now called Pinellas Point, and she regarded the whole end of the peninsula as her private reserve. It was her custom on Sundays to be chauffeured around the charming "pink streets"—so called from the original rose-colored paving that survives today—to survey her domain. A true product of her times, she ordered that no "Negroes" were to be permitted within 200 yards of the house.

The house was enormous. We had a lot of fun showing it to Joy's mother, who, each time we had moved after that first ratty apartment, had never failed to describe our new place as being "a long way from Carmine Street." We couldn't wait for her to see this place, so, bringing her in from the airport on her first visit, I said, "I just have to make a quick stop at a neighbor's to pick up something," and pulled the car up in the driveway. "Come on in, Mama."

She gaped at the house and shook her head. "Oh, no, I couldn't go in a place like that." When I told her the "place like that" was our place, I thought she was going to faint.

No sooner were we installed in our subtropical paradise than we learned the true meaning of all the Miami night club jokes about the invasions of Northerners. In eight weeks we had something like 21 guests.

There was a lot of other activity, as well, notwithstanding the sparse population. We returned from a shopping junket one afternoon to find a horsewoman and her mount peering through the window of the cat castle. Aladdin was not enjoying their visit—he'd never seen a horse before and was terrified by the rolling eyes and the snorting nostrils. I shooed the pair away and made a note to apply our next paycheck to the purchase of a chain-link fence all around the yard.

Several years passed of relative security and seclusion. Once our mengarie grew, and with it our reputation, we had more and more people driving by our property to catch a glimpse of the cats, and the occasional annoyance of someone too dense or persistent to understand that we cannot be on display 24 hours a day or seven days a week. But on the other hand we had considerate and helpful neighbors and a house and grounds that allowed us and our pets to live comfortably and quietly.

The newspapers in and around St. Petersburg came by at least once a year to do a photo story, as did the television stations. A particularly rewarding experience was an appearance on the local edition of *PM Magazine*, where we had a chance to talk about our views on the keeping of wild animals, conservation, endangered species, and the like. During the winter of 1980-1981, the local broadcast was incorporated into a nationwide *PM* show, thus giving us much greater exposure. And a major headache.

The telephone call came out of the blue, just a few days after the nationwide *PM*. A courteous but official-sounding man asked to speak to me, and then inquired, "Am I correct in saying that you are harboring wild animals on your property?" Only for the past ten years, I thought to myself—where have you been? But instead I said, yes, that was correct. The voice went on to inform me that the caller was from the City of St. Petersburg, that we were in violation of local zoning ordinances, and that a neighbor had filed a complaint about us.

I was speechless. Who would do such a thing? To the best of my knowledge most of our neighbors were delighted to have such "interesting people" nearby. If any felt otherwise, they had never expressed concern to us.

I explained to the official that when we had purchased the property in 1971 the area was zoned agricultural/residential, with emphasis on the former. "Sir," I went on, "there were horses running across my back lawn." I told him I had specifically asked about zoning and had been told there was no problem. Apparently the laws had changed in the intervening decade but nobody had questioned us, or even told us we were now in a completely residential neighborhood.

"I hate to tell you this," the man went on, and I could tell from the strain in his voice that he really had no enthusiasm for his job, "but if you don't find lodging for those animals, you'll be getting a summons." I was becoming more and more nervous about this conversation, and began trying to make the man understand that we couldn't even consider leaving our property on short notice, that we had large animals that no motel in the world would put up with for a minute. "Listen," he interrupted, "how about if I come down there and see what's what?"

The man who came to see us a day or so later was really very nice, as was the city official who accompanied him. I was never really sure what offices they represented; one was apparently from Zoning, the other from the Health Department. They couldn't fault our menagerie. "Boy," one of them exclaimed, "some people don't even keep their kids this clean."

223

But there was a definite problem. I asked about the complaint, dying of curiosity (and wrath) to find out who had done this to us. "It wasn't an individual," the Zoning man said, "it was the Pinellas Point Civic Association. That makes it rough. If one person gripes, we can usually smooth things over, but the city takes these local associations very seriously. We have to investigate."

"Are we really in violation of the law?" I asked, incredulously.

"Well, technically you are. But you've been here a long time, and when you moved in, things were different. You could get yourself grandfathered in," he mused, "but you'll have to move fast and get yourself a hearing before the City Council."

I had no idea what "grandfathered in" meant but I nodded my head and began trying to figure out what we could do . . . write a letter, get up a petition, hire a lawyer. . . . My mind was racing.

Our close friends and neighbors, Dan and Amy Schramek, moved quickly to our defense. Active in local affairs and well known in the Pinellas Point area, they were in the process of getting up a petition when they stumbled on the source of all this mischief, revealed in the civic association's February newsletter. An item on the first page was as neat a piece of innuendo as I'd ever seen.

LION ON THE LOOSE

The papers reported a pet lion loose, which had accidentally bitten a woman, and officials wished to check for rabies. The owner fled, but has been located in Pennsylvania. At the request of your Board, our Secretary has written to the City Manager, calling his attention to the fact that wild animals, used in nightclub acts, are frequently kept in our area, when the owners are in town. We recognize that these animals are exercized [sic] and trained, when they are here, to the delight of the neighbors. However, we have had complaints and housing them in the city is a violation. Our concern is that another wild animal at large might endanger our residents.

What enraged us was the implication that our (non-existent) lion had bitten someone, albeit accidentally—as opposed, presumably, to biting someone on purpose. Even worse was the picture painted of us as some sort of gypsies who were being tolerated in the area whenever we happened to blow into town.

Dan was intensely angry. "The president of the civic association," he bellowed, "doesn't even live on Pinellas Point, technically. He's way the hell down the other end, on the wrong side of Pinellas Point Drive." At Dan's suggestion we planned to attend the next meeting of the association, as our petition made its way around the neighborhood.

Joy was a wreck. She cried herself to sleep every night, and began losing weight at a dangerous rate. Confused and angry, she declined to attend the association meeting, in fear of losing control altogether, so Dan and I went without her.

These meetings can be really very unpleasant affairs. At the time of our crisis, they were almost nothing more than a kaffeeklatsch of busybodies intent on supporting any and all esthetic standards in houses and lawns so long as they agreed with their own views. They meddled well. Dan and I made ourselves inconspicuous in the back of the little meeting hall and let things take their natural course until all business on the agenda seemed to be cleared away, and then Dan stood up and said he wanted to talk about the item in the newsletter regarding the Holidays and their animals.

The president slammed down his gavel and announced the meeting adjourned, only to be met with a volley of boos and hisses from the large numbers of our supporters who had turned out for the occasion. A friend of ours who owns the local giftshop stood up and reminded the president that the residents of Pinellas Point comprise the civic association, not the officers of that august body.

The whole thing then turned into a shouting match. I was finally able to get to my feet and command a little attention, choking to fight back the tears as I told the board that they were causing my wife enormous trauma, that she was on the verge of a nervous breakdown, and that I was tempted to sue the lot of them for implying that we were a couple of ragged gypsies. Some people were crying and, feeling that I was about to join them, I walked out.

Actually, there were more than enough people in that room to defeat any motion the board might have made regarding our stay in St. Petersburg, but it was too late. The wheels of the city were in motion.

Following publicity on the evening news and in the local paper, people began coming to the house in droves to sign our petition. By the time our hearing was scheduled, for early March, we had the signatures of practically everyone in the area, some 600 names. On Dan's advice I prepared a folder full of articles from newspapers in the Tampa Bay area, the sheer volume of which was designed to demonstrate that we had never tried to keep our presence in the city a secret.

Bad publicity we didn't have, nor did we need any. The girl who worked for our veterinarian picked this time to do something exquisitely stupid on a visit to the house. She came to deliver the vet's signature for our petition, bringing along a friend who had a small baby with her. She asked to show off the cats to her friend and since Joy was chatting with Dan and Amy, I went out to the cat castle with the three of them. The dimwit was carrying the baby in her arms and should have known better—anyone who spends any time with big cats knows that small children drive them wild, probably because they perceive infants as potential playthings. In any event, she walked straight up to the tiger's kennel, and before I could stop her, stuck her finger through the heavy-duty chain link and blathered, "Now, this is my *favorite*." In a flash Herk wrapped his teeth around the finger and removed the nail and a good deal of the flesh.

I hustled the girl into the house, yelling for Joy to bring ice. As soon as calm was restored, Joy took the unfortunate creature by the shirtfront and hissed through clenched jaws, "We need this like a hole in the head right now! Don't you dare tell anyone, I mean *anyone* about this! How stupid can you be!" The assistant protested weakly that she had known Herk since he was a toddler, which was true. "But you've been around us long enough," hollered Joy, "to know that large cats would love to toss around a little baby like that!" Joy went on to threaten the girl with all kinds of horrors if she opened her mouth, and she must have made an impression because the injury was reported as a blow from a hammer and there were no repercussions.

Between the witless assistant and the upcoming hearing, we were physical and mental wrecks. Joy wandered tensely around the house, wringing her hands and muttering over and over, "Where will we go? What will we do?" As a result, on the morning of the day of our hearing, to be held at one o'clock in the afternoon, we overslept, something we very rarely do. We were awakened by the telephone and were surprised to hear a man identify himself as the driver of a mobile TV camera-crew van. He had overheard a CB message to the effect that the entire City Council, and the mayor, were planning a "raid" on us that very morning, apparently in an attempt to catch the gypsies with their miserable, dirty animals. "And, oh yeah," he added, "all three networks are on their way, too."

We scrambled. But, other than moving very quickly, we actually did nothing more or less than we normally do in the morning: Clean out the parrot's cage; check the cats for what Joy so endearingly calls "poops," and move them out of the cat castle into their daytime residences. Joy's only variation was to go out of her way to search the yard for dog droppings, something she ordinarily leaves until later in the morning. The plain truth is that if we had never known we were about to be invaded, nothing would have looked, or smelled, any different. No sooner were we dressed and the animals set for the day than the first of the TV crews arrived, with the other two hard on their heels. Less than 15 minutes later the council and the mayor arrived en masse at the door.

It was obvious that the group had been as misled by the newsletter article as the author had intended. The mayor stepped into our house with a gaping mouth, gazed around, and said, "Well, this certainly isn't what you were made out to be. This place is a palace." So much for the gypsy caravan.

The cats were in rare form that morning. In addition to sensing anxiety, they must be able to read minds, because I was hoping like mad that they wouldn't act up. They all behaved like little darlings, putting on the how-cute-I-am routines like a bunch of kittens. The mayor was delighted with them, oohing and aahing, especially when I fed them all bits of cheese and baloney from my own teeth pressed against the cages. Even Demi abandoned his practice of turning a cold shoulder to strangers and saw fit to face his audience for a change.

The city's representatives were all smiles when they waved good-bye to us, but despite their enthusiasm and their praise of our grounds and kennels, we were very frightened. Joy's hands shook constantly, and as the hour of the hearing approached she looked more and more like Lady Macbeth. Sensing that we were in no condition to concentrate on anything, Amy offered to drive us uptown to City Hall, and we docilely agreed.

At Dan's suggestion, we appeared in our own defense, bearing along the album filled with the newspaper and magazine articles. A lot of people turned out in our support, including one dear friend carrying a poster that read, "There's no place like home for the Holidays." Our next-door neighbor, who had a pair of huskies, rose to inform the council that there were worse smells emanating from his yard than from ours.

A special variance was passed, mailed to us later in the form of a certificate, honoring us as "valued citizens of the community," giving us the lifetime right to live and work as we always have, so long as we continued to maintain our property and donate our time in the form of lectures and shows for local children.

We didn't forget the people who supported us. A few days after the variance was passed, Joy wrote a moving

Joy levitating in the front yard of
the house in St. Petersburg.
(*Inset:* Cold-water walk-ups on
Carmine Street — quite a contrast.)

With Tennessee Williams and his pink Thunderbird, Key
West, 1960.

And with Wayne Newton at Blinstrub's in Boston, 1964.

Bob Goulet was the headliner when we appeared at the
Flamingo Hotel in Las Vegas in 1964.

It was probably this visit from Liza Minnelli and Lorna Luft, shown
here with Ben Vereen, that resulted in our adding illusion to the act.

Above: The Enterprise moored outside Radio City Music Hall as we arrive for our 1984 appearance in *Gotta Getaway. Below:* One of the many publicity pictures taken for that show.

Joy and Demetrius pose for some cheesecake during our appearance in San Juan.

Above: Hercules counts the fish in the pond at Alachua. *Below:* Ouch! Venus, at about 6 weeks, destroys another pair of Joy's stockings.

Opposite: Can there be any doubt that that cat is smiling?

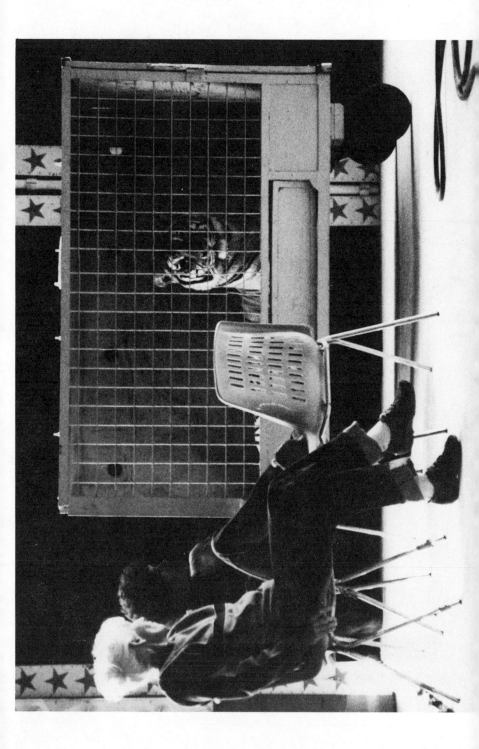

letter to the *St. Petersburg Times*, thanking the mayor, the city council, and all our friends and neighbors "for ending a nightmare that almost destroyed us."

Days before the hearing word had trickled to me from another civic association member that there had been only one "complaint" to the city, from a woman who lived at the far end of our street, on the very edge of the area encompassed by the association. The news came as something of a surprise, since only the year before this woman had attended our backyard rehearsals with her small children in tow. Now that calm had been restored, I felt compelled to go on the offensive and ask point-blank what had got into her.

I walked down the block and rang the doorbell, and realized instantly that the woman was suffering a terminal case of regret. She was probably also frightened half to death, since I was still seething with rage. The woman cried and blubbered, telling me she never meant to cause us such grief, and adding, "I'm so sorry. I didn't realize you were so famous." That struck me as about the stupidest thing I'd ever heard. Did she mean it was all right to use these tactics on people who weren't popular? Later I realized she was trying to say that if she had known there was so much support for our presence she would have laid low. Apparently she had been rather violently harassed by well-intentioned people trying to protect and defend us, and it wasn't over yet. She was receiving threatening, anonymous telephone calls. She had had her face slapped on the steps of her church. The administrator who had arranged our performance at the VA hospital years before editorialized in the local newspaper that if one of our neighbors had a problem about us, the solution was for her to leave, not us. Life must have become very trying for this woman. If I hadn't been so upset at the sight of my gaunt and nervous wife, I might have felt some sympathy.

Part of this neighbor's rather garbled explanation of her behavior included a fear that her young children would wander the three long blocks to my property, scale

229

the five-foot Cyclone fence, and be attacked by the cats. This was so patently ridiculous I was at a loss for a response. The woman had been in my yard. Hadn't she noticed the huge, reinforced kennels that contain my animals? Did she think I just let them wander around the grounds? "Besides," I added, heatedly, "anyone who climbs over my fence is in no danger from the cats. My guard dogs would eat them alive . . . and they're *legal!*"

Weeks later I received a long, rambling letter attempting to clarify our conversation on her doorstep, the essence of which was that she suffered from childhood with a phobia about tigers. The key ingredient in this phobia was a recurrent dream in which a tiger jumped through her bedroom window and devoured her. She claimed she would never have purchased the house so near us if she had known that we possessed a tiger, but considering that she had summoned the courage to sit on my lawn less than a dozen feet from the uncaged animal, this argument made little sense. Whatever the real reason, she certainly turned our lives upside down for a few weeks.

There is a factor here that cannot be overlooked. On several occasions people who know us well have related to us fairy tales told by service and delivery men. Some individuals simply cannot resist a little self-aggrandizement by telling "gee-whiz" stories about their visits to our property. One friend told of encountering a telephone repairman at a party who, when our names came up, proceeded to recount in living color a well-embellished narrative about coming through our gate unexpectedly one afternoon and finding Joy standing in the backyard with Hercules . . . loose. There followed the usual "Boy, was he big," and "God, was I scared," and the like. Our friend, recognizing a piece of fiction, questioned him closely but he stuck to his story. Perhaps, if I give our phobic neighbor the benefit of the doubt, she also heard a story or two like this. If only these trades people realized the damage they do when they spin these yarns. . . .

The truth, obviously, is that on no occasion are the animals ever closer to being "loose" than on the end of a stout chain or leash. Even at night, when they are led from the kennels to their indoor sleeping quarters, they are held on short leads very close to us and for as brief a time as possible. It is almost a certainty that, after all these years, we could just open their kennel doors and point to their cages, but we will never ever take the chance.

3

Not too long after our harrowing experience with the City, we decided to act on a desire to escape Pinellas Point. Much as we loved the house, its nearness to the water, and our neighbors, and much as we had killed ourselves physically and financially to turn the place into a protectorate for our animals, the area was just becoming too crowded. Our phone rang constantly with people wanting to come around at the darnedest times to see the cats, some of them hanging on the fence trying to catch a peek at them, a practice that drove our guard dogs wild.

Perhaps one of the most severe problems was the location of the cats' kennels, along the back wall of the cat castle. This was the shady side, under the branches of an enormous mango tree, but it was also the side that could not be seen from the house. This situation always bothered us, but its potential hazards were brought home to us dramatically one afternoon when the housekeeper of a neighboring residence rang our doorbell to say she thought something was wrong with Hercules. The big dummy had been swinging around on a huge truck tire hung from the center of his kennel, had snagged a tooth in the rubber, and was nearly unconscious after a futile struggle to free himself.

We wanted more room for the cats—habitats, really, instead of the kennels—and more privacy. So, two years after fighting so hard to stay in our home, the house went on the market, while we combed the northern, less developed part of the state for some significant acreage we could afford.

We have always kept a tidy house. Joy is one hell of a housekeeper, and I am a fanatic about my yard looking trim and neat. We didn't expect too much difficulty in selling our historical home, but interest rates were high and so was the price for all those rooms and that big lot, so time went by and we had scarcely a nibble. And then we had a real disaster, one that set back our prospects for a sale by several weeks.

The central heating system that Mrs. Tippetts had installed in her palace by the sea was an expensive and inefficient albatross that we avoided using as much as possible. The house was so big for the two of us that we inevitably ended up heating rooms we didn't use. Over the years we learned how to get through some pretty awful winters with only the fireplace in the solarium and the odd kerosene heater in the kitchen and bedroom. Joy is terrified of space heaters of any kind and always insisted on shutting them down whenever we were out of the house. But Christmas week of 1983 was particularly bitter, so when we dashed out that Sunday for more firewood, we left the heater in the kitchen running, turned down as far as it would go and set in the middle of the kitchen floor where (we thought) it could do no damage.

When we returned, I opened the front door and yelled, "Hey! Who turned out the lights?" The interior of the house was pitch black and it took me a moment to realize that it was filled with smoke. The kerosene heater had decided to eat itself for lunch, and when the fuel ran out it spewed forth enough smoke to cover every surface of almost 5,000 square feet with a quarter inch of soot. Pepe, in his cage by the kitchen window, was unconscious; I had to rush him into the back yard and shake him vigorously to bring him back to life. He coughed and evacuated black gunk for three days. How he survived at all is something we'll never understand.

No one who hasn't lived through something like this can fathom what it means to have not one clean object or corner in the house in which to escape the dirt. The stuff had slithered under the doors of the closets and coated our clothes, towels, linens, toilet paper. Lampshades, picture frames, carved wood molding on furniture, the nooks and crannies of the coral fireplace, the tiles in the showers—everything was sooty. On the afternoon of the fire we could stand in the middle of the house and the stuff would settle on us like a fine, black snow. For three days, until the company hired by the insurance carrier came to start the monumental clean-up, we didn't bother to shower or change our clothes. It would have been pointless.

It took six weeks to set the place right, including a complete rebuild of the kitchen, which had been virtually gutted by the heat. Even the telephone had melted off the wall.

But, when it was all over, we had a virtually redecorated, renovated house, right down to the beautiful hardwood floors, and the place sold. When we finished our nostalgic return to Radio City Music Hall in the summer of 1984, we moved directly to our new 16-acre property near Gainesville.

4

Most of this story has been told from Ron's point of view because he takes care of our "internal" workings—and this book has been a sincere attempt at an inside view of our lives. But now I want to wind up our story by talking about Ron and Joy Holiday, citizens of Planet Earth. I guess I got elected because, as should be obvious from Ron's descriptions of my willingness to leap into any fray, I've become the voice of the team to the world, the one who writes the letters, talks to the newsmen, and raises Cain when I see an animal being abused. It is an unfortunate fact of life that many of the people who are responsible for the wellbeing of captive creatures simply don't give much thought to what that responsibility entails. There's a lot more involved than just a square meal or two every twenty-four hours and an occasional pass at making the cage look presentable.

We may "own" jungle cats in the technical sense, but in fact we are nothing more than caretakers of these animals, providing food, shelter and love, and doing the best we can to merit the trust. Wherever we live, we at-

tract attention—there aren't many people who can ignore a neighbor who shares his bed and board with a
tiger—so it would be inexcusable not to seize the opportunity to spread the word. And the word is, essentially,
we share this planet with all living things, and all living
things must be respected.

I often think about the literally thousands of people
who have sat in our driveway on all those Saturday
mornings and watched us perform, and of the questions
they have asked and the answers I have given. I like to
think that the hundreds and hundreds of children who
have passed through our gate have been made aware of
the fragility and sanctity of life, of the fact that an exotic
animal is not just some pretty conversation piece to be
picked up, thoughtlessly, at a pet shop, enjoyed while the
fun lasts, and then cast aside.

When we aren't on the road, I like to respond to re-
quests from schools, parent-teacher organizations, service clubs, and the like, to talk about our animals and
the work we are involved in to preserve endangered species around the world. Speaking at schools, or having
school children make a class visit to the house, is a job I
undertake with relish. The kids are a captive audience
as they sit hypnotized by the sight of the cats, and there
is no better time to remind them that animals feel pain,
that animals need love, that each has its own needs and
personality, just like people. I always ask them to draw
me pictures of what impresses them most, when they get
back to class, and send them to me. It's fascinating to see
what turns them on. The youngest are always awed by
the cremation, when I climb into the big mirror ball and
Ron sets it aflame. And when Venus flies through the air
into Ron's arms. (Often they get confused and write to
say how they loved it when Ron caught the jaguar in his
arms. Being around our animals all the time, we must
be like people who live with twins: Only the parents can
tell them apart. To us, the difference between a 90-pound
Indian leopard and a hefty, 200-pound jaguar is obvious.
Still, innumerable newspaper reporters have stood in

our yard, interviewed us, watched the show, been introduced to the cats, and then gone back to their desks and perpetuated in print the very same mistake. Suffice to say that Ron is big and Ron is strong, but Ron could no more catch a leaping jaguar in his arms than fly to the moon.)

We have saved every thank-you letter and every picture delivered from these kids to our mailbox; they make wonderful reading, often touching, often amusing. Just how important these class visits are, and how grateful the schools are for them, was brought home to us by one kindergarten teacher who wrote to point out that virtually every corporation she had approached for a class trip, such as the local power and telephone companies, had turned her down because such a visit would be "dangerous." "In comparison to your show with the four big cats," she said, "I really feel unsympathetic to their attitude." One wonders what sort of operation these powerful companies are running that they think their facilities present more danger to children than eyeball-to-eyeball contact with a tiger.

Newspapers, radio and TV people come to interview us regularly. We have a scrapbook stuffed full of clippings and photographs from these occasions. The media may think they've got a good human-interest story when they give us a big color spread in the newspaper or an appearance on a local TV talk show, but the real benefit is that another few thousand people can get a good look at a wild animal and gain some understanding of what that animal is all about.

We are lucky enough to be in a position to talk to many, many people under relaxed and informal circumstances, people who come willingly and with enthusiasm to see us and the cats. But it didn't take us long in our careers to start looking beyond our own back yard. Among the responsibilities we shouldered with our permits to keep endangered species was to become interested and active supporters of groups who are trying to protect those animals.

One of the first bits of our consciousness that got raised when we first began working with the cats was that many animals kept in captivity are not happy and healthy. Most large zoos do very well in this area, although even with the best of facilities and professional personnel they have had to think and rethink the way they do things. Once the industry got over its initial tendency to stick all wildlife in small, cramped cages, there was a move to the other extreme—great, wide open spaces. This was not necessarily a good thing. An animal must feel that it can escape, not just from something, but *to* something. Some animals, stuck out in vast plains in what purported to be a "natural habitat," surprised the professionals by becoming not fat, lazy and content but extremely nervous and disoriented. More consideration is being given now to smaller, more sheltering environments.

But if the zoos are doing great work in conservation and preservation, there are thousands of miserable creatures in "road-side attractions" who suffer untold agonies every day. Poor diet, improper shelter, airless habitats, lack of companionship are the norm for these animals. There is a movement under way to wipe out these atrocities, a movement in which we have been very active, and we hope the day will come soon when any so-called "animal attraction" will be forced by law to provide proper living quarters and professional veterinary attention for its captives—or be put out of business.

Another group of animal lovers, to which we also belong, is trying to ban the possession of wild animals as pets. There is a statute moving through Congress, slowly, which would make it illegal to keep any rare or unusual creature unless the owner can prove he or she is making a legitimate living, as we do, from the animal. Such a law would put an end to the deformed monkeys who are constantly being brought into zoos because the owner didn't know how to keep it when he bought it and then didn't know how to undo the damage caused by poor diet and a cramped cage. And to the great snakes that people release, willingly or not, to terrorize neighborhoods until they are recaptured or killed. The average person can just barely manage to care for a dog, a cat or a canary; he shouldn't be allowed to wring the life out of an exotic animal for the sake of his own ego.

It goes without saying that our "pets" are far more to us than a source of income. Each of them is a treasure. They are our children and our friends, creatures who give us comfort and entertainment, for whom providing care is a privilege and a joy. We love every inch of them, from their wet, rubbery noses to the tips of their long, furry tails. We have to hope that the day will come when all animals, exotic and ordinary, wild and tame, will be granted their rightful place on this planet and be able to thrive in the sheltered contentment that ours enjoy.

Epilogue

The rehearsal over, and the animals starting to slide into their afternoon siestas, the crowd gradually drifts away. Car engines start up, and a cloud of dust follows the caravan back down the road. A few people don't want to leave. They stand in mute rapture staring at the tiger, as if trying to carve his image forever in their minds. The tiger, accustomed to this sort of thing, yawns mightily and settles down into the grass of his kennel. The show is over.

While I close the gate, Joy goes into the house, waving over her shoulder as a final hint to the stragglers. "Goodbye! Come again!" Most of them will indeed come again. Some of them never miss a performance.

People always ask when we'll call it quits. We see no reason to do so, not as long as there are jobs and as long as we can keep our shapes and our fitness. If the day of retirement ever comes, we're ready. We have a long list of animal behavior studies we want to do. There will be other cats and dogs to raise, perhaps even a new and unique animal to add to our menagerie, and there will be organizations and committees to join for the protection of all of earth's creatures.

We are learning all the time. With each animal we discover a new personality, different habits and requirements, varied training methods. What works for one cat fails on another. We want to go on doing this—raising and loving our animals, performing with them with the flashing lights and the stirring music, experimenting with training techniques, talking to anyone who will listen about conservation—for as long as we can, and for as long as we're wanted. And we'll let the animals go on training us—as long as we're willing to learn!